COUNTRY LIFE
IN SCOTLAND

COUNTRY LIFE IN SCOTLAND

Our Rural Past

ALEXANDER FENTON
National Museums of Scotland

JOHN DONALD PUBLISHERS LTD
EDINBURGH

Tibi

ISBN 0 85976 188 6

The cover illustration, from a
photograph by the author, shows
Mrs. Peter Leith, outside the
byre at Appiehouse, Stenness,
Orkney, in the 1960s.

Reprinted 1989

Phototypeset by Quorn Selective Repro, Loughborough, Leicestershire.
Printed in Great Britain by Bell & Bain Ltd., Glasgow.

Contents

Introduction: People in Change

This book is about people. It is about people in a countryside where the horse ruled supreme. What has happened to the people of the countryside over the last two or three hundred years? How have they responded to changes that were more often than not forced upon them? What changes have there been in their working lives, in the tools and equipment they used, in the houses they lived in? In the chapters that follow, a single theme is being looked at. It is complicated and has many ramifications, for it reaches into the heart of our existence. It has to do with age-old, inbuilt rhythms of life that became, after centuries of little-varying routines, an instinctive part of the psychological make-up of country dwellers. Here may lie the roots for which so many people are searching today.

In Scotland, the process of disruption started nearly three hundred years ago with the beginnings of industrialisation, new trading developments, urbanisation and agricultural improve-

Farm folk at Blairmaud Farm, Banffshire, about 1927. Per Robert Ewan. C909.

At Charlie Gray's farm roup, North Pitglassie, Auchterless,
Aberdeenshire. AF, 1973, 51.57.10.

ment, all these things going hand in hand. In the modern world,
there are countries where such living rhythms have only just been
broken, often in a crudely revolutionary fashion that will create
generations of unrest. The Scottish experience is a longer one.
There are elements of evolution in it as well as of more drastic
change. There are messages for now, for other parts of the world, in
the story of Scotland and of her country people over the last two
centuries.

Though Scotland is a small country with a population of just
over five million, she still has an important place in Europe. She
divides the North Sea from the Atlantic Ocean, and along with
Ireland, holds a pivotal position between the cultures of Northern
and of Continental Europe. Her resources in coal and in iron-ore
led to important industrial developments including shipbuilding,
and the wealth of fish around her coasts has long attracted the
attention of other European nations. Sea-links with the countries
around, and contacts across the Border with her larger neighbour
to the south, to which she was joined by a union of Crowns under
James VI of Scotland, and I of England in 1603, and by a Union of
Parliaments in 1707, have left a mix that is reflected in language,

Left, A Shetland lass. Mary Jamieson, who looked after her parents at Biggins, Papa Stour, Shetland. AF, 1967. 53.15.1 and right, the late Miss Mary McArthur, descendant of an old farming family at Coillebhraghad. near Inveraray, Argyll. AF, 1982. 53.15.7.

literature and lore, songs and music, art, buildings and monuments, and tools and equipment, as well as in forms of administration and law. All of these blend to make the elusive concept of national identity, the feeling of being Scottish.

At the present time, over three quarters of the population is concentrated in the industrial and urbanised Central Belt, but the farther back we go in time, the greater was the number of people living in the country. In 1755, over 51% of the population lived north of the Central Belt. The Southern Uplands, with 11%, was rather thinly settled. The remainder was in the Central Belt itself. A century later, the proportions were 33%, 9% and 58%. By 1951, the Central Belt had 75% of the total for the country, the north 20%, and the Southern Uplands 5%. There was a strong flow into the industrial centres. At the same time, though, there was general growth in the size of the population. It should not be thought that the north and south were left more empty. They also shared in the growth, but the industrial centres grew faster. Overall, there were more people in the countryside in the 1950s than in the 1750s, and this is a fact that should not be forgotten.

The wedding at Nairn in 1919 of Alex. Matheson, farmer at Tighnahinch and Dunvournie, Easter Ross. Per Miss D. Matheson. C6592.

An important part of the history of Scotland is the difference between Lowland and Highland areas. The Highlands were different in language and culture as well as in economics. After the administrative Union of 1707, lairds and businessmen in the Lowlands were able to look for economic opportunities in association with the vast markets of England and her colonial empire, to the growth of which Scots contributed much. As a result, through agricultural improvement, invention, and technical innovation, Lowland Scotland came to be a dynamic sector of the economy of Britain as a whole.

The Highlands, or more exactly much of what we now call the Crofting Counties, fell farther and farther behind. In the late eighteenth and nineteenth centuries a great deal of effort was put into trying to make the most of what they had to offer. Seaweed was manufactured into the alkali, kelp, for use in soap and glass-making. Commercial forms of sheep-farming were introduced. Deep-sea fishing, deer-forests and forestry were developed. The fortunes of these activities came and went, but in the end, along with forestry and fishing, the grazing of stock has continued to be

An old couple,
Auchterless,
Aberdeenshire. C9350.

the main base. This is barely enough in itself however, and extra means of earning a living are needed, as postman or roadman, and through catering for visitors. Since the 1880s, Government grants have played an important part in keeping people going. Many are distributed through the Highlands and Islands Development Board, and have an unconcealed underlying social purpose.

The broad differences between the Highlands and Lowlands are not the only kenmarks of Scottish identity. There are several distinct regions, marked out by differences like geography, types of farming and dialect. The South-West goes in for dairying. It has much in common with Northern Ireland, and has had a lot of influence on the Inner Hebrides. The East and South-East are grain-cropping areas, where advanced farming with a European reputation was practised, and where important innovations like the swing-plough, threshing machine and reaping machine were developed. The North-East, one of the most densely settled areas in Britain, was marked by the rearing of stock, especially cattle fed on the great acreages of turnips that were grown, until these began to be replaced by silage and other alternatives. The Highland and Island emphasis was on stock-rearing, with the drama of the heavily-publicised 'Clearances' forming a historical backdrop. In addition, there was the strong and enduring influence of the big towns and industrialised areas. Their demands for food led to greater milk-production, pig- and poultry-rearing, and horti-culture in the countryside around, all helping to provide for the basic food needs of the multitudes as well as delicacies like fresh strawberries in season. These distinctions are just as important as the Highland-Lowland divide in looking at the country as a whole.

Wherever possible in the chapters that follow, the illustrations have been chosen to show people, posed and unposed. Even when posed for the serious business of the photograph or for the formal occasions of life, people tell us much about themselves through the way they stand, the tilt of their bonnets, the thumb in the galluses. The pictures are to be read as much as the text, and the text is a background to the pictures that often catch the mind vividly with the flavour of changing times.

Sandy Macpherson, the postman at Lochailort. M. E. M. Donaldson, about 1920. 51.13.12.

CHAPTER 1
Deep-Ingrained Rhythms

Except in a country like Albania, where Government policy is to maintain a stable population in the countryside, the usual result of the growth of industry has been to draw people in from the country to the town. The early development of industry, in Scotland as in England, depended on water power, and there was not too great a degree of disruption at first, since industry had to go into the country to find its source of power, and workers could straddle two worlds, still clinging to their home base.

With the adoption of coal as the main source of power, industry became concentrated where facilities and outlets lay most conveniently to hand. When this point was reached, the real break with the old days had begun. This break was so fundamental that its deep psychological effects lived on.

What was its scale and nature? To get an impression of what the deep-ingrained rhythms of earlier times were like, we cannot do better than to look at the diaries of farmers kept during the period of horse-draught before technological innovations like the tractor

Feeding hens in East Lothian in the 1920s. Per Mrs. Cockburn. C4859.

Carrying loads on horseback and on the human back in the 1690s, at Culross, Fife. From Slezer, *Theatrum Scotiae*, 1693. LIB/1593.

began to shape the countryside for the new twentieth-century revolution that has come upon it. In such diaries, it is remarkable that there is no comment on the unchanging daily routine tasks, such as the feeding of poultry and milking of cows by women, and the mucking of byres and stables and feeding of horses and cattle by men. The weekly routine marked by regular visits to market and church is touched on, but the main concern is the work in the fields, the winter ploughing, the making of a tilth in spring to give seeds a good bed, harvesting the hay, grain and root crops, and preparing these for fodder and for sale. There is a strong annual rhythm, with peaks of intensity at seed-time, harvest, and during ploughing, and slacker periods in June and August. The rhythm is in truth even longer, for there is really no such thing as a farming year. It continues through the whole rotational cycle, which may run for three years or more till the same crops are back in the same fields again. Centuries of farming by a population that was overwhelmingly rural up till the end of the eighteenth century must have burned such rhythms deep into their souls. It is little wonder that a sudden and almost mass transition to industrial work came as such a profound shock to the system that many failed to adjust. It is hard, in an instant, to do away with the built-in rhythms of centuries. Change to the strict, unvarying daily routine of a factory was a mental shock. An antidote might be looked for in drink and other social evils.

There were other kinds of traditional rhythms. An ancient one was to be found in the Crofting Counties, the Borders, and in all

Back transport by a standing
stone at Uyea, Shetland, 1890.
Per Lady Linda. C12971.

Lowland areas adjacent to the hills. It was marked by the summer
movement of stock for grazing from the lower ground to the
higher, and their autumn return. The use of summer shielings,
where women and young folk looked after the cows and young
beasts, and processed the milk during several glorious open-air
weeks, lasted longest in the Outer Hebrides, especially Lewis,
where many people of middle age still remember the life. The
flitting relieved pressure on home grazings, and gave crops a
chance to mature without the need for constant herding.

The shieling huts grouped in the hills belonged to the houses in
the farming villages sited on the low ground by the coast or in the
straths or valleys. So tightly were the units bound together that the
shieling huts could be called the 'summertown' and the parent
village the 'wintertown', as if they were elements of one and the
same village. The use of hill grazings was so much part of a
long-perfected subsistence economy, little if at all based on money,
that the separation of the two was almost unthinkable. Yet when
money-based economic pressures led in the late eighteenth century
to the introduction to these areas of commercial breeds of Blackface
and Cheviot sheep, often with southern shepherds to look after
them, the traditional economy with its need for summer grazing

Conditions in the towns were wretched. At 39 Overgate, Dundee.
C10020.

was well and truly broken. Survival was made more difficult and
complicated for the native inhabitants. Their hill grazings had
been taken from them to make way for sheep, and their villages had
been moved from straths to less hospitable coasts in what came to
be known as the Clearances. Even though areas of common
grazings were allocated to them, these were but faint reflections of
the grazings they had before. This was no less a revolution than the
drawing power of industry in the more central country districts,
with effects that were at least as extreme in their own way. Another
deep-ingrained rhythm was broken for ever.

A widespread but younger rhythm was the seasonal movement
of workers from outlying to central areas for harvest work. Such
short-term annual migration goes back to the later 1600s and
continued until the invention of the reaper and binder made it
unnecessary. By the 1700s, weekly markets for shearers were firmly
established in East Lothian. Highland shearers were being hired in
thousands at the West Port in Edinburgh and elsewhere by the end
of that century. Most of those from the Highlands were young
unmarried women, who carried their sickles and bore large
bundles on their backs. Sometimes they moved in family groups.

House-servants at Corramore, Argyll, 1910. Per Hugh Cheape. C4901.

They went chiefly to the high-farming areas of Fife and the Lothians, and some also to Angus. This rhythmic Highland-Lowland flow continued until cheap fares in steamships allowed Irish workers to start coming in very great numbers to shear the southern Scottish hairst from about the middle of the nineteenth century. There was also a lesser flow of shearers from North-East Scotland to the south, and some small tributary movements such as that represented by a day-labourer in Glenesk who walked to and from a farm at Laurencekirk to work at the harvest each year in the 1870s-80s.

But the main rhythm of seasonal migration was the ebb and flow of Highland shearers. It seems to have begun as a growing population created pressures in the North and West, and as agricultural improvements gave rise to an ever-growing need for workers to secure the bigger acreages of better crops in the Lowland cropping areas. The flow was reduced and finally blocked by seasonal Irish migrants; and after nearly two centuries a major source of income for Highland families disappeared. The result was a worsening of the problems they had in plenty in their home areas.

Milking a cow at a shieling in Lewis, before 1928. C1229.

Traditional rhythms like these contrast sharply with factory work, and their disruption for people who worked on the land contrasts also with the rhythms of life of the lairds and ruling classes, which continued to flow on without interruption. Many of these could also be described as seasonal migrants, like Mrs Elizabeth Grant of Rothiemurchus who, in the early 1800s, annually flitted between south and north with the family in a carriage, whilst the servants travelled by sea, taking even furniture with them. At this social level, it is difficult to speak of absentee landowners, for the landowners moved from estate to estate, from London house to Edinburgh house or Highland house, and were at home in familiar surroundings wherever they were. The Industrial Revolution and the Agricultural Revolution brought no special break in their seasonal rhythm, but rather improved the possibilities for easier movement into increasingly comfortable quarters. They maintained a strong degree of continuity in their undisturbed attitudes and outlooks, whereas the bulk of the remainder of the population suffered a harsh break in their traditional mental and work rhythms. Inevitably, the distance between the two levels of society became sharper and the degrees of difference hardened. The roots of what would now be called working-class consciousness were first bedded in this post-

Nannie Egan, an Irish shearer, reaping wheat with a sickle near
Corstorphine, Edinburgh. S. Salmon, 1890s. Per Miss R. S. Cowper.
C1755.

industrial estrangement.

The breaking of basic, traditional rhythms of working and
living, here or in other countries, leads to massive social change.
These rhythms went on irrespective of the course of history and the
coming and going of kings, for they were based on the need for food
and the provision of homes. They were disturbed from time to time
by the effects of weather, as in the Seven Ill Years of 1696 to 1703
shortly before the Union, or by the fortunes of war, but they were
very persistent because the way of life was based on them, as in
Afghanistan where people have tended crops by night in areas
continually under threat of devastation by day. The human race
may be the most adaptable of all living creatures, but its instinctive
rhythms are just as deep as those of other creatures. It takes time to
replace them, once broken, and the nature of the kinds of
replacement can be various, and strange.

CHAPTER 2

The Old Community: A Lesson In Survival

It is common nowadays for parts of estates to be sold off, often to meet the cost of State-imposed death duties, and a new breed of owner-occupiers of farms is growing. Formerly, however, splitting off of parts like this was unthinkable. The estate was the base for the organisation of almost the entire countryside. Its home farm or mains farm supplied the needs of the 'big house'. Other farming units, large and small, were let to tenants, and there were supporting services like the meal-mill, smithy, joiner's workshop and sawmill. The exact nature of what made up the estate varied according to the type of farming economy imposed by the physical environment.

In pre-Improvement days, before the Agricultural Revolution got into its stride, estate organisation was more closely in line with other countries of Europe. Farming activities were based on farming 'villages' whose arable fields were not worked in

Runrig fields beside Arbroath in the 1690s. From Slezer, *Theatrum Scotiae*, 1693. LIB/1585.

An earthen or *fail* dyke being replaced by a post-and-wire fence, near New Deer, Aberdeenshire. AF, 1966. 53.14.65.

individual blocks, but on the run-rig system. This meant that a group of farming families, often perhaps interrelated, was running a farm jointly, each family making use of a number of scattered strips and patches of land which might be changed around between them from time to time. This is what some scholars call 'tenant run-rig', in contrast to 'proprietorial run-rig', though the difference lies only in the fact that not only tenants had intermingled pieces of land, but landowners also. In other words, there was a community system within the bounds of the estate, and estates themselves could also form part of wider community systems.

Since forms of land-use were conditioned by the need to get food and also to produce the extra needed for rent in money and provisions for the landowner and his family and officials, it is important to understand how the land was organised then for production, before later improvements based on enclosing, sub-division of fields and draining had completely changed the social structure and the appearance of the face of the land. The kind of rhythmic pattern of work imposed by secular or church forms of administration, themselves shaped largely by the available means of exploiting the available resources of the countryside, was

Wet area at the edge of a runrig field, brought to light after clearing a wood at Auchterless, Aberdeenshire, and now reclaimed for cropping but not systematically drained with tiles. Fields in the old community often looked like this. AF, 1970s.

severely strained before it settled into new forms. It was not only a question of traditional rhythms being broken by the pressures of industrialisation, but also of a range of changes taking place in these very rhythms before industrial developments began to put their dominating stamp on the economy of this and other countries.

In pre-Improvement farming communities, the run-rig units were divided into infield and outfield. The infield, also called croft-land or mucked land, was the most productive land, nearest to the houses, manured with some regularity, and planted with a wider variety of cereal crops than elsewhere, mainly oats and bere (a form of barley). The cropping sequence was bere on the manured unit of the infield, followed by two years of oats without manure, and then back to manuring and bere again. There could also be a more complicated sequence that included wheat, which was manured too but not as heavily as bere. In such a case, the infield was in four units rather than the more widespread three. This situation, found for example at Hallyards in Midlothian in the 1660s, marked the better farming areas where improvements were eventually to make the most rapid headway.

The outfield was a more extensive area whose function was to provide general resources like turf for a multiplicity of uses and close-at-hand grazing, as well as crops of oats. It was divided into a greater number of units than the infield. Every year a temporary turf dyke was thrown up around one or more units, and the interior used as a fold for stock, so that their droppings could manure the ground for a crop. Other parts were left fallow after cropping for as long as it took for a sole of weedy grass to regenerate. For these reasons the outfield could also be called the folds or the faughs (fallows).

Both infield and outfield were marked by the characteristic broad ridges and furrows made by the old plough, giving the impression of irregular corrugations. They are still to be seen, a landscape made by man and horse and ox, on the lower slopes of the Pentland Hills, in the Lammermuirs where traces of twelfth to sixteenth-century cultivation and settlement lie high in the moorland core, and in isolated pockets through the country, as where old ploughland has been fossilised by conversion to a golf course or by the planting of trees. They remain also on lower-lying ground that is difficult to drain, except by surface drainage in the furrows between the ridges. Many examples can be seen from the train windows on each side of the railway line, on both the Scottish and English sides of the Border. In light snow and slanting sunlight they show up well as images of long-past days.

The third element essential to the farming community, alongside the infield and outfield (or what passed for these in Highland and other areas where the terrain was difficult), was the rough grazing or moorland amongst which the arable patches and thatched houses of the units of settlement were everywhere islanded. This was, like the outfield, an essential service area. It provided grazing near-at-hand and remoter shieling or hill pasture areas, as well as peat for fuel, and turf for building dykes and house walls, for lining house roofs under the thatch, and for mixing with household refuse and animal manure in the earthen compost middens that all the farm folk made and regularly turned as a means of eking out the scarce supply of fertiliser.

The pre-Improvement farming system was not as primitive as later writers with the flush of new-day spirit in their blood made it

An earth midden or *mooldiekoose*, held down by stones as a protection from the wind, in Foula, Shetland. AF, 1958. 51.57.7.

appear. It was a highly-sophisticated, long-evolved response to environment and resources, and knowledge of how to manipulate these was in the blood and in the bone of the people of the time. Except for years of famine or other disasters, they knew how to survive.

They had developed a kind of ecological cycle that could conserve resources, as long as it was not pressed too hard by factors like population growth. The infield and outfield produced bere and oats for ale and meal, and straw for fodder and for thatch. The infield was manured by animal dung from byre and stable, droppings, rotted household refuse, and composted earthen middens based on turf cut with flauchter spades in outfield and moor. The ash from the peat fires went into the middens directly, or by way of the byres where it made a useful sponge for soaking up urine in the bedding. Collapsed turf walls, decayed turf and thatch from roofs and earthen or fail-dykes damaged by the hooves and horns of stock all followed the same path. The grass and weeds and young shoots of hill plants fed the beasts in summer without any special input from the farmer, and were converted into meat, milk, butter and cheese, manure, and wool and skins. There was an

A compost midden of seaweed and byre manure, in Papa Stour, Shetland. AF, 1967. 53.14.1.

energy flow. The resources of the environment were channelled and converted through the stock and through domestic uses into nitrogenous material that helped the crops to grow better, and they in turn produced food and drink and fodder of which a goodly proportion found its way back into the cycle. The surplus from the two elements around which all life revolved — crops and stock — went into feeding and clothing the family, foddering the stock in winter, paying the rent, buying what was absolutely necessary, like the ironwork of the plough and flauchter spade blades, and covering the cost of essential services like mill and smithy. What went outside the system was the rent to the laird (some of which could be returned in the form of his obligation to provide, for example, roofing timbers for the houses), and the scarcely quantifiable cost of manpower for services such as work on the land of the home farm, the carting of fuel, etc. The main return was that the work ensured permission to live on a particular patch of ground.

These elements of the old farming community dictated the rhythm of the work of the year. A marked feature of it is symbolised by the word 'community' itself. The families in the farming villages shared a unit of land which was divided out in parts

19

amongst them. Much collaborative effort was necessary. Tracks were needed across the ground of neighbours for access to strips and patches where work was to be done, and loans or loanings along which cattle moved from the byres to the grazing areas. Herding was a matter of joint concern, as were water supplies. The main need, however — for which good neighbourhood was required — was the sharing of animals, whether horses or oxen, in making up the teams of six, eight or more animals required to draw the heavy 'old Scotch plough', and cultivate the high-backed ridges. Few farmers had enough draught-animals to make a full team. Community work was the solution, especially at a period when ploughing stretched over a greater part of the year than it came to do later, and when sowing and harrowing (for which a further pair of horses was needed) had to be done at the same time as the last of the series of ploughings that had broken in the soil, turned weeds under, and finally prepared the seed-bed. It is a mark of community feeling that the herd-boys, who later could grow up to become ploughmen, would have known the oxen from birth, registering all their foibles and physical characteristics, and giving their charges names to match, like 'Brandie' (brown with a stripe across the back), 'Cromack' (crooked horns), 'Hakey' (white face), 'Humly' (hornless), 'Garie' (striped or variegated on back or sides), 'Belly', 'White-Horn', 'Gray Horn', etc. Such familiar knowledge was a well-established part of the deep-rooted working rhythms of the old farming community.

CHAPTER 3

The Farming Community: Muck And Corn

The old farming community may have looked static, but all the same it was subject to long-term change which can only be assessed by looking back over half-centuries or more at what the Civil Service would nowadays call performance indicators. These could include the nature and numbers of stock, the quality of houses, furnishings and equipment, and perhaps, above all, the actual spread in areas of settlement. This spread is best seen in areas like Sutherland and Banffshire, where former grazing areas in hill valleys, after generations of manuring by the droppings of stock, came under the plough and became centres for new farms. This long, slow evolutionary process was reaching its final stages by about 1750 to 1800.

For the most part such changes came from within the community and remained in line with its natural working rhythm. Later writers, fired with improving zeal, speak of the backwardness of pre-Improvement farming and blame the conservatism of the

Driving out heavy loads of dung, using box-carts with trace-horses to ease the strain, at Strathmiglo, Fife. Per Hugh Cheape. C537.

A large lime-kiln at Ardneakie, Sutherland. AF, 1970. 53.10.13.

lairds for it. However, the lairds were as much in the hands of the environment and its resources as their tenants. It is likely that what in the end enforced a more revolutionary set of changes was the fact that the land's resources had been driven about as far as they would go, in relation to population growth, by the early 1800s or earlier, depending on place.

The search for advances in manuring techniques was part of the effort to improve returns from well-used arable areas. In 1595 Archibald Napier, son of the inventor of logarithms, wrote a pamphlet called 'The New Order of Gooding and Manuring of all Sorts of Field Land with Common Salts', which dealt with salt as a manure, and an intricate system of folding animals for the better manuring of land. Of much greater general importance than salt, however, was the use of lime, which, though long used for building purposes, was surprisingly not appreciated as a fertiliser until the 1620s, and then at first only where limestone outcrops occurred near the coal that was needed to burn and calcine it in clamps and in kilns. The Lothians and Ayrshire led the way. Besides producing better yields of oats, liming was also a means of extending the arable acreage in outfield areas, and of bringing the outfield up to infield standards. This led to a great increase in land under the plough. Liming was sometimes overdone so that land

Substantial stone dykes separating individual crofts, running from the sea to the hill, at Durness, Sutherland. AF, 1970. 53.14.63.

was made unproductive for a time, but the first flush of liming enthusiasm has left its mark on the lower slopes of hills in the Lothians, Borders and elsewhere, in the form of cultivated ridged-and-furrowed fields that afterwards reverted to grazing only. These remain as monuments to an attempt to extend resources that succeeded only in part, since it was not yet accompanied by systematic underground draining. That was to come only two centuries after lime was first applied as a fertiliser to outfield crops of oats.

The results of outfield liming could still be contained within the system. It did not at first affect the infield, which was the hot core of the old farming community, except in the more naturally fertile areas where a fourfold infield cropping sequence of bere, oats, wheat, pease, rather than a threefold one of bere, oats, oats, could, by the 1660s, include a year in pease manured with a little lime. This was still within the limits of the old system.

Such efforts reveal growing pressures on the system, however. There were also outside pressures that eventually brought it to bursting point. In national terms, it was not sufficiently productive for the country to be able to do without a considerable import of Baltic wheat and flour. The Government, no doubt

A dyked enclosure or *stell* for sheep-working, in the Borders. AF, 1970s. 53.10.9.

alarmed by the flow of money out of the country, greatly reduced the level of Baltic imports in the later seventeenth and first half of the eighteenth centuries, though supplies from England and Ireland may have helped to make up deficits.

One question, however, is whether or not there were deficits. Certainly by this period, the risk of periods of scarcity had become relatively low, and technical factors like the use of lime were extending both the acreage and quality of crops. Furthermore, Scotland had herself begun to export Lothian and Moray grain to Holland, the Baltic, Norway and Western Sweden, getting timber supplies in return, and to England also after the Union of 1707. There was a much increased coastal traffic in grain, after about 1660, from the northern parts of Scotland to the capital whose mills and breweries processed it into food and drink, and whose merchants sent it on farther. This trade was based on contracts offered by merchants to landowners for their annual crops and annual rents paid in the form of grain. Market forces, therefore, were creating pressures for the production of grain as a commodity from the arable areas of Scotland that could be turned into capital.

These forces were encouraged by a Government with liquidity problems, which protected grain producers by prohibiting or

The old croft dykes are replaced by government subsidised post-and-wire fences, at the village of Arnol, Lewis. AF, 1973. 53.14.61.

controlling imports, and by putting a bounty on exports. It acknowledged a need for improvement in the productivity of the land which was its major national asset, by a series of Acts such as those under James VII and William and Mary relating to the enclosing of land, the division of commonties, winter herding and a drainage scheme at Inchaffray in Perthshire.

What these pressures meant in terms of the living standards of the tenant farmers is hard to assess, except by inference from later days. Legislation opened the way for what in the end was a wholesale reorganisation of the farming pattern and of rural society, and for changes in land use and layout that, taken together, do indeed justify description as an 'Agricultural Revolution'. Concern to maximise grain production was the primary motivation in the mainly Lowland arable areas. Change within a legislative framework was quickly followed by technical innovations like new types of ploughs and threshing equipment.

In these areas, enclosing was the most prominent mark of the new era. It was not an unknown phenomenon earlier, for in seventeenth-century Galloway and in East Lothian, enclosed grazing parks were established to fatten cattle for the market. The use of earthen dykes as temporary fold walls, and substantial stone dykes too as markers of territorial boundaries (some old enough, as in parts of Orkney, to have been partly buried under the growth of peat), was also common. What was quite new in the eighteenth century, however, was the building of reasonably permanent walls and the planting of hedges to enclose individual properties, individual farms, and the fields within them. Thorn or beech hedges could be combined with ditches, and stone dykes absorbed stones cleared from the fields. When Lord Belhaven published his booklet on *The Country Man's Rudiments, or An Advice to the Farmers in East Lothian how to Labour and Improve their Ground,* in 1699, he barely mentioned enclosure. Thirty years later, in 1729, when William Mackintosh of Borlum wrote his *Essay on Ways and Means of Inclosing, Fallowing, Planting, etc. in Scotland,* the enclosing movement, having got its bible, may be said to have begun, leading to the kind of farming landscape with which we are now familiar and which differentiates Scotland — and other parts of Britain — from the great, unenclosed field systems of most other European countries.

CHAPTER 4

The Shieling Grounds: Grass And Cattle

Parts of the Crofting Counties, notably Easter Ross, and parts of the South-West, developed in line with the most advanced farming practices of the Lowlands, and became grain producers in the same way. Generally speaking, however, cattle formed the key element in the economy of the Crofting Counties.

Seventeenth-century economic factors led to a sharp increase in the sale of black cattle to markets in England. Cattle became one of the country's staple exports, helping to feed the rapidly growing city of London, for example, and the army and navy. Scotland kept England supplied to such an extent in the century before the Union of 1707 that Mackintosh of Borlum described her as 'a mere grasing field to England'. One of the visible results of this trade was the appearance by the 1680s of dyke-enclosed cattle-grazing parks near Edinburgh, and in Galloway through the trading activities of lairds like Sir David Dunbar of Baldoon. Other results, though less tangible, were more far-reaching. Their character varied in the different pastoral areas. They are to do with the breakdown of the shieling system.

Economic pressures expanded the acreage under crop in parts of the Lowlands, though without at first breaking the ancient farming system. So also did they lead to greater use of the hill shielings, without immediately disrupting the annual rhythmic movement of the Highlanders between low ground and high. The first sign of change took the form of intensified use, when lairds sent their black cattle to the hill, but still allowed the mixed stock of their tenants — sheep and goats as well as cattle — to go there too. For a time the traditional pattern of land use through summer shielings co-existed with estate-organised hill grazing, but increasing competition between the mainly subsistence needs of the tenants and the market-orientated activities of the lairds was inevitable. However, as long as the focus of attention was cattle, the shieling system was able to survive, partly because tenants were also producing cattle which in due time became part of the droving trade to the south.

The story applies also to the glens of Angus and North-East

27

The old kind of circular, bee-hive shaped shieling hut, at Uishal,
Lewis. AF, 1970. 53.14.49.

Scotland. In the seventeenth century, the small heritors of Glenisla
went to the glens bordering on Braemar to graze their cattle in
summer, living there in small, circular huts of turf which they
threw down when they left. In the high-lying parts of Banffshire,
the system was closely controlled by the estate in the seventeenth
and eighteenth centuries. It was partly domestic, for tenants had
the right to graze a certain number of sheep and cattle in the hill
pastures. Cattle were an essential part of the tenant economy on
farms lying at levels too high for good crops of grain to be easily
grown; the profit from them could buy extra meal, and help to pay
the rent.

Dovetailing into the domestic system was the practice of estate
herding. Lairds sent up herdsmen, as their paid employees, a week
or two before the stock, to keep off cattle from the shieling grounds
of neighbours, and the many horses that roamed freely, so that the
grass would be at its best. There were similar arrangements in
Sutherland and Inverness-shire. By employing herds, the lairds
ensured full use of the shieling grounds, though the basis of
production remained the family or farm unit, paying rent in cash
or kind or a mixture of both. In these areas, however, the spread of
cultivation through the breaking in of well-fertilised shieling areas

The later kind of rectangular shieling hut, built of stone and covered with turf on the outside, at Glen Mór Barvas, Lewis. AF, 1971. 51.57.25.

had opened cracks in the system by the 1780s, though it continued in a modified way.

Perthshire had its own characteristics, in part due to the distances between the parent farms and the shielings, which could be up to twenty miles away. This could lead to the use of an in-between shieling area, just beyond the head-dykes, to which stock went when the first spring grass appeared. Later in the year, the major move to the distant shielings took place, so making the best possible use of grazing resources through a two-stage movement.

There were often also two stages in the sending out of stock. Young horses, dry mares and animals not needed for work went a week or two in advance, along with herd-boys who had a glorious time in the freedom of the hills. This was the 'small flitting', when the summer huts were repaired after the winter storms, re-thatched, and stocked with peat fuel. Young heather was pulled and packed in tight, upright bunches into the bed spaces, to make a fragrant, yielding mattress for tired limbs. The milk cows and the women arrived later at the time of the 'big flitting', when everything had been prepared and made snug for them.

Recesses for milk vessels in the inner stone wall of a shieling in Glen
Mór Barvas, Lewis. AF, 1971. 53.14.51.

There was also an out-of-season use of the shielings. Herdsmen
remained in the huts during winter to look after *yeld* (dry) or young
cattle or horses, which got the full freedom of the grazings after the
milk cows had gone. This practice, known from Glenlyon in
Perthshire in 1725 as well as from Caithness, and no doubt
common enough elsewhere too, helps to explain what happened to
cattle that there was no room to house in the byres during the cold
months. In this way the hills were grazed to the maximum, and
there was less pressure on the grazing at the parent farm or village,
so that pickings remained for returning animals. It was important
for their survival that, except for occasional bad periods, the
relatively mild climate of the West allowed grass to keep growing
for the greater part of the year.

The very remoteness of some of the Perthshire shieling grounds
was a factor in the breakdown of the shieling system here, and
already by the end of the eighteenth century the custom had begun
of joining two or three such areas together and letting them as
grazing to a shepherd, who took up residence on the spot in a
substantial house of good masonwork, often with a blue-slated
roof. These units became separate sheep-farms, with names like
'Newton' pointing to their relatively recent origin.

In most places, shieling-grounds were grazed in common by the stock of those who had a right to use them, but in Assynt in the north of Scotland, individual grounds were enclosed by dykes. In the 1760s, the 246 recorded Assynt shielings were divided among forty-two joint-farming communities, each with its own bit of the pasture. Eventually many of these units of grazing became partly arable crofts.

This was not like the permanent extension of the settlement pattern into shieling areas that took place in North-East Scotland, however. The change in Assynt was more of a compromise, a kind of halfway house. The allocation of croft units to individuals, in fact, lasted only as long as the cattle were grazing there, and as long as patches of corn were being grown. When these had been harvested, the ground reverted to being common grazing. There was a problem, however, because the corn-growing period was longer than the families' normal period of stay. The solution was for poindlers to be hired. They began work in April to deal with stray animals, and moved from shieling ground to shieling ground guarding the corn from the eager jaws of ruminants. The Badenoch people in Inverness also employed poindlers in the 1760s to look after their grass. They were equivalent to the Banffshire herds.

It appears from a survey of Assynt, carried out by John Home in the 1760s, that corn crops were regularly grown at the shielings and were of good quality because of the animal droppings. In Argyll, Ross, much of Inverness and Perthshire, shieling grounds lay at higher levels and cropping was impractical. However, the cropping of the Assynt shielings undoubtedly emphasises the anxiety; people had to keep themselves in meal.

The variations in different districts show that there was not a single 'shieling system' but a number of variations which had evolved over long periods of time to suit local conditions. What was generally true, however, was that people everywhere felt that the time of going to the shielings was one of delight, a highlight of the year, to be spoken of afterwards with nostalgia. The excitement of the move made hard work a pleasure.

In the Western Islands, there was a sequence in the pilgrimage: sheep travelled first, then the younger cattle, then the older cattle and the goats, if there were any, and lastly the horses, laden with all the necessities of existence. The men went at the same time,

carrying spades, timber and ready-twisted heather ropes to repair
the huts. There were places like mainland Argyll where the
precious roofing-timbers were brought home and taken back again
each year. The women were probably more heavily laden than the
men. They carried blankets for bedding, the dairy utensils and
oatmeal for the daily porridge. They also had spindles and distaffs
for spinning wool, and it was often during the lazy summer days at
the shieling that young lasses were taught the art of spinning by
their elders. To let them walk more freely, the women kilted up
their long skirts with a belt, and in spite of the burdens on their
backs they knitted stockings as they walked along, no doubt with
their tongues hard at work as well. In mainland districts like
Perthshire light peat carts could carry the loads, and spinning-
wheels were also taken, as well as swatches of woven cloth that were
bleached during the time at the shieling. Another job for the
women and sometimes for the herd boys when they were on the
hills was the gathering of roots, herbs and lichens for making dye.
A lot of work was done on textiles at the shielings, including much
of the preparation of yarn for weaving, which was a usual winter
job.

In the Hebrides especially, the movement almost had the ritual
of a solemn ceremony. There was the formality of checking each
family's allocation of stock by the village officer or constable. This
was the souming, the number they were allowed to graze. For the
sake of working out souming equivalents, units of stock were given
certain values, i.e. 1 cow was equal to 5 sheep, and 1 horse to 2 cows
or 10 sheep, as at Arnol in Lewis. People could graze whatever
stock they liked, as long as the total did not exceed their allocation
of units. When the checking was done, fires were lit in the freshly-
prepared huts and a meal was prepared, often with cheese, and a
prayer could be offered up and a hymn sung. The men then left for
the village or wintertown, there to see to the hay-crop, to tend the
other crops in the unfenced fields, to repair and re-thatch houses,
and to tan leather to make shoes and harness. Many also went off
from the Highland and Island areas for a season at the
herring-fishing.

The shieling system declined as a result of several factors. In the
valleys of mainland Scotland, the spread of cultivation played a
part. Much more important, however, was the course of agricultural improvement itself, which brought to an end the old

Ferrying Highland cattle in a boat at Kyleakin, Skye. C1882.

farming community system, with its common use of arable and grazing resources. Where the process of enclosure had been completed, and each farm-house with its outbuildings stood in the midst of its own individual fields, there was much less need for shielings. Improved cropping techniques, the use of sown grasses, the better processing of hay, and, after the 1750s, the rapidly increasing use of turnips as winter fodder went far to make the new farm units self-sufficient for the whole year round. They could manage without shielings.

All the same, the value of hill grazing is well recognised. Many Lowland farmers also run hill farms, with close working links — overwintering of stock on the lower ground, etc. — between them. But the units belong to individuals and the workers are paid employees. It is very different from the old community movement of people and stock. In general, the conversion of shieling areas into hill-grazing farms has characterised the edge of the eastern Highlands of Scotland since the end of the eighteenth century.

In the central and eastern Highlands, there was an intermediate phase, when the hills were used both as shieling grounds for the small farmers and as hill grazings. This kind of double use goes back at least to the early eighteenth century in mainland Scotland and might be older. It is certainly older in Skye, where, in the seventeenth century, the demand for Highland cattle by dealers from the Lowlands had already started to force along changes. First of all, the traditional time of return from the shielings at the beginning of harvest had to be brought forward to mid-August. This was to suit the dealers, who came to the cattle fair that was established in Portree in 1580 to get beasts for the fairs at Falkirk and Stenhousemuir in mid-September. The animals had to be swum across to the mainland. It is likely that in support of this trade, the grazing of herds of black cattle on the hills and moors of Skye was going on alongside the summer grazing of the stocks of individual families, even by the early sixteenth century. It is known, for example, that cattle for winter slaughter were already being exported to the Lowlands by that period.

Joint use of the hill grazings went on for long in Skye. When John Blackadder surveyed the estates for Lord Macdonald in 1798-1800, he summed up the view of the time on local economics: each farm should grow enough grain so that the farmer did not have to buy more in the market, and the grazing or yearly value of the cattle should pay the rent. Both crofter and laird recognised the importance of cattle, and the Skye pattern was not unlike that in Strathavon in Banffshire: that is, it was a mixture of domestic and commercial. At the same time, it was the emphasis on trading in cattle that gradually brought about change in the old shieling system in these areas, allied, perhaps, to population increases that enforced increased use of any available resources, including those of the hill. When this happened, commercial interests could hardly fail to knock against the old, domestic shieling system.

Nevertheless, in Skye and in the eastern Highlands, change was at first evolutionary, with intermediate stages that allowed the ordinary tenants to adapt to some extent. What finally ended the shieling system, however, was the massive introduction of commercial breeds of sheep, Cheviot and Blackface, when both hill grazings and former settlement areas were emptied of their former inhabitants and users to make way for the sheep of the gentlemen. Large single-farm units were created, and leased to sheep-men, many of whom came from the Borders of Scotland. They could pay much higher rents than the displaced native farmers. This 'Clearance' period came mainly in the nineteenth century, and reporting in newspapers was vigorous enough to leave a strong mark on the national consciousness. Sheep-dykes on the Galloway pattern, loosely built so as to make adventurous sheep uncertain about trying to jump them, appeared in the Highland landscape, and these, as well as the posts and wire and equipment connected with later fencing, have left their mark on the technical vocabulary of Gaelic speakers.

The one interesting exception in the story of the Clearances that ended the shieling system is the island of Lewis, where shielings survived well into the twentieth century. There were not many evictions there to make way for sheep farmers, partly because the Seaforth lairds had not been willing to turn people off their holdings in the early days of the sheep-farming boom, and because the laird in the second half of the nineteenth century, Sir James Matheson, maintained a paternal approach to his tenants. But this is not the whole explanation. During the period 1755-1801, the population increased by 139% as against 48% in the Highlands as a whole. At the present day a high number of farming units is under ten acres, and of these many are under five acres. No other area has such a large concentration of small units. Self-sufficiency is, in practical terms, impossible. Outside means of earning income are necessary, but earlier on, community activity was vitally necessary, as was access to shieling grounds. Whatever the reason, or mixture of reasons — and these must include the rough, boggy terrain that made the island difficult to exploit for sheep-farms — Lewis remained the last surviving shieling area in Britain.

Until the introduction of intensive sheep farming, change in the Highland communities was most evident in the adaptations in use of the shieling areas, designed to improve their productivity in cattle for trade. It was a natural, reasonably evolutionary form of development, parallel in kind and in emphasis to the outfield expansion in Lowland areas, and to the growth of the trade in grain there. Highland cattle and Lowland grain, therefore, produced finance for the lairds who were eager to invest in farming improvements or in the early forms of industry based on water power. These twin economic supports helped to provide the capital essential for such ambitions. It is ironic that the improvements resulting from the resources channelled from all parts of rural Scotland, themselves led to the disruption and eventual destruction of the old traditional rhythms, ending the mental stability of centuries.

CHAPTER 5

New Days: The Work Force

Trade in grain and cattle was by no means the only source of money for improvements, but it affected the countryside most. What of the consequences of the improvements themselves, regardless of how they were financed?

There was much moving around of people, in different ways. The replacement of the old communities by individual farms meant that many members of such communities no longer had any stake in the land, even if this had been as slender as a widow's right to graze a cow. This was, in a sense, their form of social insurance. The rationalisation of the old communities into separate, enclosed farms led to a double movement.

First of all, a farm-worker class developed to serve the needs of the farms. They became paid employees, with wages partly in cash and partly in kind. They were no doubt often the farmers and members of the families of farmers who had been displaced by the improvements, and who had not been able to scrape together the

Proud of his pair. Dave Colville at Hayston Farm, Balmullo, Fife, 1928. Per A. Barron. C7451.

rent required for a new holding.

Secondly, there was a movement into the small villages that appeared in the Scottish countryside as part of the improving movement, which was by no means confined to farming only. People from other countries find it hard to imagine a countryside almost without villages, but this was true of Scotland until the later eighteenth and nineteenth centuries, when lairds expanded the existing few villages or created quite new ones. The purpose was to promote domestic industries like weaving, lacemaking,and snuffbox-making, as well as fishing and water-powered industry. Over 150 villages were born in the 1700s, scattered through the country, places like Simprin and Castletown in the south, Cuminestown, New Byth and Huntly in the North-East, and Halkirk far north in Caithness, still marked by the great regularity of their layout in their original cores. These added quite a new element to the landscape of settlement. They were an essential complement to the shaping of new farms, for they absorbed a great many of the displaced population, whilst still allowing them to live near to the areas they had known from birth. They provided reservoirs of day-labourers, and of additional workers during intensive work-periods on the farms.

The growth of new villages was also a phenomenon of the Highlands and Islands. Fishing ports like Tobermory (founded 1788) started up, but of much greater social significance was the resettling of groups of people moved from the glens to the much less hospitable coasts as a result of the Sheep Clearances. There, the houses of the new farming villages often lay in a line along a track, with fields stretching below them down to the sea, and a head-dyke at the top of the arable to separate it from the common grazing area. These farms reflected the new outlook, because they lay each on their individual strip of land; but the shared grazing pointed back to the old days of a more far-reaching community structure.

Another kind of movement, an important one for which no statistics can now be got, arose from the fact that the process of land settlement was far from complete by the eighteenth or even the nineteenth century. Though new, improved farms might be shaped out of infield and outfield areas, there remained around them vast areas of unreclaimed moorland and waste ground. One of the major outlets for people disturbed by enclosure, approved of and fostered by laird and tenant farmer alike, was the resettling of

Three pairs in front of the cartshed at Kirkton of Collace, Kinrossie, Perthshire, in 1928. Per H. Davidson. C7392.

families on patches of land at the edges of moors and peat-bogs. Little or no rent was charged for the first few years, but the occupants had the herculean task of breaking in the inhospitable ground and clearing stones with spade and pick and might of arms, till the patches were reclaimed and productive. The farms alongside gradually absorbed these reclaimed units, in countless numbers, from the beginnings of improvement. The process is still going on, for example with the small farms or crofts of North-East Scotland.

The movements mentioned were of such a kind that the people stayed in the countryside, even if not always directly on the spot where they had been brought up. Their age-old rhythms of life were broken, certainly, but perhaps only in part, for they remained within reach of the old associations. It was otherwise with the multitudes who flooded to the towns of Scotland and of England, to work in environments that were totally strange. For them, the rhythm was fully broken, but reorganisation of the countryside left no alternative other than to leave it. Overseas migration marked the aftermath of the Clearances in the Crofting Counties. However, those who reached the New World could still take up the well-known rhythm of the farming year as they occupied new ground there. Similarly, the many people with trades needed in the new country, who migrated from the Lowland counties of Scotland, could continue more or less where they had left off. For some time, leaving aside the difficulties and dangers of crowded sea-journeys, emigration may have been preferable to the unvarying routine of work in smoke-filled factories.

What were the effects of change at farm level? We can assess these by making a comparison with the composition of the labour force in the mid-seventeenth century. According to an Assessment of Wages, drawn up by the Justices of the Peace for Midlothian in 1656, there were four broad classes: a whole hind, who was required to maintain an able fellow servant, so that between them they could see to the work of a plough; a half hind, or single man; a shepherd, who also had to maintain a servant; and a tasker, who threshed grain with the flail. He could be employed full-time on big farms, or for a few weeks at a time on smaller ones. The wives of all these were expected to work too, and their work was understood as paying the rent for the cot-houses in which they lived. It was no light task that the wives had. The Assessment laid it down that they were to shear daily in harvest until their master's corn had been cut down; they had to help their husbands at the hay and at the peats, in setting the lime-kilns, gathering, filling and carting muck and all other kinds of material that could be used as a fertiliser, carrying stacks from the barnyards to the barns for threshing, fetching food for the stock from the barns to the byres, cleaning the byres and stables and winnowing the corn.

Besides these married servants, there were unmarried plough-men, farm lads, female servants and maids, who lived in or received their food in the house. Whereas married workers were paid partly in money and partly in kind, the single servants got food and board plus a money wage.

The first major change was that those working on farms, other than members of the farmer's family, became hired hands. The second was that the composition of the labour force began to change as technological improvements came along.

Improved plough-types like James Small's swing-plough, patented in 1767, could be worked by one man standing between the stilts and controlling the pair of draught-animals with reins. Formerly, teams of six to ten or even twelve oxen had been used, with one man to control the beasts and another to control the plough. The new cultivating technology brought an immediate saving in both man and animal power. In part this was made possible by better and stronger breeds of horses, like the Clydesdale,

A box-cart outside Dundee in the 1690s. From Slezer, *Theatrum Scotiae*, 1693. LIB/1583.

which began to be widely bred in South-West Scotland, and sold in early February at Lanark Fair and elsewhere. It took part in stallion shows in Edinburgh in 1757 and 1783, and its systematic breeding is said to date from this time.

As the use of such strong horses spread, so also did the improved ploughs, and improved forms of one-horse carts. The results at farm level were very marked. To take an example from Monikie in Angus, a farm there used five ten-ox ploughs in 1750, and only three four-horse ploughs by the 1790s. This reduced draught-requirements from fifty to twelve, and manpower from twelve to at least six. In the next parish, Muirhouse, a farmer cut his staff from thirteen to six over the same period. These are great savings in economic terms; but the servants who became surplus to requirements had to leave, to tackle the daunting task of taking in a croft from the waste on their own account, or to swell the villages, towns and cities, or to emigrate to worlds unknown.

Ploughmen or horsemen, the hinds, became increasingly skilled members of the hierarchy of farm workers. Others, however, disappeared from the count. A noteworthy example was the tasker. He was also called the barnman or lotman, because he got as his wages a lot, or twenty-fifth part of the grain he threshed.

On smaller places all men did their own flail-threshing, as one of the most frequent elements in the regular routine of work. It absorbed a huge amount of time and manpower. The more the acreage of crops increased, the harder it became to deal with them by hand. It is little wonder that the search for quicker means of threshing was eager, and Andrew Meikle's threshing machine of 1786 brought a real revolution in its train. The barnman, before then one of the most important members of the labour force, rapidly vanished from the farming scene as the impact of the mills made itself felt. He was the first of the old-style servants to disappear.

Next came the replacement of whole hinds simply by married hinds, who no longer were required to maintain an able fellow servant to help with the plough. This change, already clear by the 1790s, must reflect the widespread use of improved ploughs with small teams, that required one man only to work them.

The shepherd continued to be an important figure. In the Borders, it was reckoned in 1797 that he was £2 a year better off than the hind, though this was in part due to the fact that he was given the yearly keep of a number of sheep as part of his wages. This was worth more than money, it seems. The system continued, and even in the 1960s Border shepherds still kept a pack of thirty-six breeding ewes and nine hogs as an element in their wages. This was the breed of men who were to provide the skills needed to look after the kinds of sheep with which they were familiar, when sheep farms were established in the Highlands. Shepherds were not, of course, equally prominent in all parts of Scotland.

Though part of the farm-servant range disappeared, other types also came into being. Some were not part of the full-time force, but probably came from the villages and towns. Amongst them were hedgers and ditchers, who by the 1790s were getting wages equivalent to those of shepherds. This is beyond doubt a mark of the amount of effort going into the remodelling of the farming landscape, giving it the shape with which we are now familiar.

Reorganisation of manpower and of the farming system led to a need for management policies. Accordingly, a new class that first appeared in South-East Scotland was the farm grieve, overseer or steward. Some of these came from Northumberland, across the Border, where agriculture was already highly advanced. By about

Lowsin' time at Pusk Farm, Fife. Per A. Barron. C7478.

1754, three farms in the parish of Swinton and Simprin were occupied by the Northumbrian stewards of three Northumbrian farmers. They were said to have maintained a certain social state and degree of aloofness, whereas the native farmers were hardly to be distinguished from their servants in dress, attitudes and eating habits.

There seems to have been lively activity in the Borders because of the high wages on the English side, which meant that the South Scottish farmers had to pay more to keep servants. Living standards amongst them were rising. They were said to have an alert, busy look, and their womenfolk, to the great annoyance of the parish ministers, were buying more expensive kinds of dress, including silk, and indulging in the new 'pernicious habit' of drinking tea. The area was about a generation in advance of elsewhere in Scotland in these respects, by about 1800.

In these high farming areas, too, it was especially common to have tied female outworkers on the farms, comparable to the tied dairywomen of the pastoral South-West. They were often called bondagers. They were the wives or female relatives of the hinds, or were supplied by the hinds as part of the hind's condition of employment. There was some outcry against the obligation of hinds to provide outworkers, and an attempt was made to organise East Lothian ploughmen against it in 1845. This failed, but the custom petered out in any case by the 1860s.

43

All the same, the use of women outworkers on big farms did not fade quickly, neither here nor in other areas like Fife and Angus, and not even as far north as Caithness, though they were no longer tied as they had been earlier in the century. They were distinguished by their characteristic dress, which has come to be described as 'bondagers' dress'. On their heads was a wide-brimmed hat of black, plaited straw, with a rim of red rucheing. The brims were tied down in a fold at each side. They wore a neat blouse and drugget skirt, a striped apron, and boots buttoned up the sides of the legs. When the fields were muddy, as during wet work amongst turnips, they wound straw ropes round their ankles up to their knees, and 'breekit' their petticoats by fastening them between their knees with pins. Though women outworkers were to be seen in the fields until recent times, their clothing had become modernised. A special kind of headgear remained, however: no longer the plaited straw hat, but one of cloth, with a light wicker frame forming a wide hood in front, and a flap at the back, to protect the face and neck from wind and rain and sun. They were a little more pleasing in appearance than the Lothian name 'ugly' and the Lanarkshire name 'crazy' would suggest.

The new kinds of farm units, from the second half of the eighteenth century onwards, required a fixed labour force with its own forms of internal organisation and standards. There was, of course, a close relationship with the available technology and the functioning of the farms in general. Ploughing took up a great part of each year, and continued to do so. From October of one year till March of the next, it went on without respite, and outside these periods also. The ploughman, therefore, was a most important figure in the work force. He was also the horseman, who looked after the horses that provided the chief motive power. Depending on the size of the farm, which was often reckoned by the number of horses needed to work it — a 'twa-pair place', 'fower-pair place', etc. — there were the 'first horseman', 'second horseman', and so on.

The general change by the 1770s from oxen or cattle beasts to horses for draught, gave a great boost to the prestige of the horseman class. As part of the very real spirit of excitement of the period, bodies like the Highland and Agricultural Society of Scotland were founded (1784), and numerous local Agricultural Societies followed soon after. Over 130 had come — and sometimes

A pair at Kincaple Farm, Fife, with a 'long-cart' or harvest cart in the shed behind, in 1922. Per A. Barron. C7444.

gone — by 1835. These greatly encouraged ploughing matches and harness competitions, and helped to foster the pride in their horses and their turn-out that became part of the horsemen's way of life. As a side issue, professional saddlers and harness-makers came into existence in the towns around the 1790s. It was the farmers, of course, who bought their products, and not the men, but in later times, at least, there was much circulation of pieces and sets of harness from farm to farm as a result of farm roups or sales, which gave smaller places a chance to kit out their horses at less expense than if buying direct from the saddler.

There was also the cattleman, who spent much of his time cleaning, feeding and otherwise seeing to the cattle in the byres, and there were young farm-servants, the halflin's or orra-loons, who joined in all the jobs to be done and looked after the odd or unpaired horse and worked with it. A strict hierarchy came into being. At jobs like the hoeing of turnips, the grieve took the first hoe and the halflin' the last, with others in sequence in between. The same order was followed in going into the farm kitchen at meal times. Different areas had different categories of workers: for example, in Roxburgh there could be a plooman steward and a foreman steward, and it was the plooman steward who kept the time and set the pace.

Working through and alongside this hierarchy was the question of married or single status. Some areas had a preference for married servants, and others for single servants. Preferences could vary from time to time, and sometimes there was a mixture. Figures for the 1840s, for example, show that the strongest preference for married servants was in the high-farming districts of the South-East and Fife. Single men, on the other hand, were preferred in Caithness, throughout most of the Crofting Counties, and in North Angus and Kincardine.

There were differences in mobility between the two groups, especially in the Lowlands. Right down until the period of recent memory, married servants moved every year from the cottar-house of one farm to that of another, and single men changed masters every six months at the feeing-markets. These differences also affected the nature of their accommodation, for single men, and sometimes women outworkers, might live in bothies in which they saw to their own food, or in chaumers in which they slept only, getting their food in the kitchen of the farm where they worked.

A category about which little is heard was the day-labourer. Displacement of people as a result of agricultural improvement left a large reservoir of spare hands in the towns and villages. They were called on to work at day-rates at periods of peak intensity on the farms, for example at the hay- and grain-harvests, when the fixed labour force could not cope alone. The role of the day-labourer — in alliance with or instead of seasonal migrant workers from the Highlands or from Ireland or from North-East Scotland — was to provide an essential support to the farmer, without which he would have found life much harder before the days of plentiful machinery. The history books have still to acknowledge and evaluate the importance of the day-labourer in the rural economy.

The shaping of the new farms, neatly enclosed and with fenced fields worked in an established rotational cycle, led to an annual farming rhythm that did not differ so much from that of the old community, except that it was more structured in terms of management, and had a definite market orientation. It was a rhythm that involved winter ploughing, the daily feeding and cleaning of animals, the weekly driving of stacks to the barn for threshing, an intensive round of ploughing, harrowing, sowing and rolling in spring, the driving of muck to the fields, the opening

A saddler at work in Edinburgh, at the St. Cuthbert's Co-operative
Society. AF, 1970s. 53.10.5.

and mucking of drills for turnips and potatoes, the hay and corn
harvests, the long-drawn-out pulling of turnips in the cold days
when the beasts were again indoors; and, especially in the higher-
lying areas, there was the seasonal round of work with sheep.
Whatever the regional variations, it was a strong, identifiable, and
certain rhythm, which was, in itself, the outcome of the work flow
in response to the seasons and to the rotational cycle.

CHAPTER 6

Small Farmers And Crofters

A group which should not be forgotten is the large number of crofters and small farmers who personally cultivated the lands they occupied, helped mainly by members of their own family. The group originated in various ways. From the early beginnings of Improvement, there were the small tenants who took up small areas of land, in what were then marginal areas, in order to reclaim them. They, as well as artisans and tradesmen who had small holdings near town and villages, practised a kind of subsistence farming combined with part-time employment, which could itself be farm-work in the form of day-labour or part-time labour. The shoemaker, the gravedigger, the molecatcher, all had their crofts. Even the ministers had their glebes, and schoolmasters had patches of land, which were also intended to eke out their incomes.

In East Central Scotland particularly, the pendicle became very common. This was a small piece of ground held by a sub-tenant who was either a tradesman, or who paid rent for his holding by working for the farm to which it was attached. The 'crofts' of North-East Scotland were comparable. Untold numbers grew out of the process of reclamation, and were later absorbed into farms, a process which still goes on. At the same time, there has been a long

Jimmy Tawse, a 'crafter' at Hill of Hatton, Auchterless, Aberdeenshire. Such small farmers often had other jobs. Here he is catching moles on a neighbouring farm. AF, 1970s. 3.14.32.

A Harris crofter and his wife putting out the cows after milking.
AF, 1971. 53.14.53.

tradition of mutual help also between bigger farms and smaller places, which supplied essential additional labour to the farms at busy times, and were themselves then helped in turn. For a time, at least before mechanisation totally altered the economics of farming, they also fulfilled a valuable social function, for they could give a first foothold for those of ambition who wanted to climb the farming ladder.

The main area for crofts, however, is in the North and West, in the seven Crofting Counties of Shetland, Orkney, Caithness, Sutherland, Ross, Inverness and Argyll, where a legal form of crofting tenure exists. This was established by the Crofters Holdings (Scotland) Act of 1886. Its essential features as established then and subsequently modified in minor ways are:

   a. Security of tenure as long as the crofter pays his rent and complies with various statutory conditions.

   b. The right to a fair rent. If there was a disagreement, the amount was to be fixed by the Crofters Commission established in 1886. Fair rents are now fixed by the Scottish Land Court.

c. The right to compensation, on leaving, for permanent improvements provided by the crofter or by the predecessor in the tenancy.

d. The right to bequeath the tenancy.

In 1886, the upper limit of rent for a croft was £30. This was raised to £50 in 1911 under the Small Landholders (Scotland) Act. In size, a croft ranges up to about seventy acres of inbye land, and the crofter has the right to graze his stock in common with other crofters in the township (group of crofts), on an area of common grazing.

Given this legal base, there remains a great variety of conditions within the Crofting Counties. They include some of the most prominent farming districts of Scotland, such as Orkney, Easter Ross and the parishes of Cawdor and Moy in Inverness, and areas with great numbers of tiny holdings, such as Lewis. Over time there has been a range of forms of occupation of the soil in these counties, including holding by tacksmen who had leases from the lairds and sublet to smaller tenants; bowers who had grazing farms for milk cows; steel bowers who according to the old steelbow form of tenure received their stock and cattle along with the ground, and had to return the equivalent when they moved; pendiclers, who, in the north, usually held their pieces of land from the chief tacksman; cottars, who had a house and portion of land but no cattle, who worked for a farmer and had their land tilled by him; dryhouse cottars, who were labourers with no more than a house and kailyard; and crofters in an older sense of the word, who controlled their own arable but had their cattle herded and looked after with those of the tacksman. The result of the Crofters Act was to level out such variations, which, in general, marked the better parts of the Crofting Counties, as well as counties like Moray which lay just outside them. The range is conditioned by a mixture of bigger and smaller farming units and their working relationships. It could not exist in areas where holdings were uniformly small.

In 1886 legislation effectively limited or prevented any growth in size of crofts in such areas. At present the number of crofts is around 19,000. Of these, no more than 5% provide full-time agricultural employment. The rest must find additional sources of income. Besides, because of the small scale of operations, a form of community life is still necessary, though it is much altered from

An Orkney crofter's wife, near Stromness, feeding a motherless lamb from a bottle. AF, 1960s. 53.15.37.

the older rhythms, when annual summer migrations to the shielings took place. Sheep-shearing and dipping, and peat-cutting, for example, all require joint effort if they are to be done expeditiously.

The scale of community effort varies also from place to place, and in relation to croft sizes. In Wester Ross with 816 crofts below 5 acres and 287 between 5 and 10 acres, the need is much less than in Easter Ross. There, only 84 crofts are below 5 acres and 85 between 5 and 10 acres, and big farms are common. They provide employment for crofters and easy outlets for sales of stock. The most intensively occupied crofting region is undoubtedly Lewis, with 2,299 crofts of under 5 acres, 1,022 between 5 and 10 acres, and only 19 over 30 acres. It is here that the shieling system lasted longest, probably because there were few possibilities for expansion of a kind that would have produced alternatives to the need for the summer grazings in the hills.

Conditions of life in the Crofting Counties make specialisation difficult, and an ability to mix skills is necessary. A man may work on the land one day, or may be at the fishing, or shepherding, or gamekeeping, or house-building, or road-repairing the next, all with equal facility. In terms of class structure, too, they have special characteristics. There is not a diversified social structure. The landowners at one end and the crofters at the other have few or no gradations to separate or link them. There are no grieves or foremen to act as intermediaries, as between the farmers and men of the farming areas. The womenfolk play a considerable role in the work of the crofts. Indeed this role increased after the development of the herring fishing began to take the men away from home at times when work in the fields was needed. Nevertheless, they have never had any specific status like that of the bondagers of South-East Scotland. On the other hand, crofts do not have the 'landless' labourers of the Lowlands, although this relative freedom was gained at the price of having a stake in the land that was often worth less than the wage earned by a Lowland labourer. That is mainly why the Highlands and Islands Development Board has to see its grant-giving as a social function.

CHAPTER 7
Farmers And Men

No system is perfect. There are good and bad masters and good and bad servants, and most have a bit of each from time to time in their constitution. Occasionally an agricultural writer has had a look at the farmers themselves. G. S. Keith, writing from Aberdeenshire in 1811, spoke of three classes of farmers, who may be taken to characterise all the main farming areas at that time.

There were the old native farmers who enjoyed blethering to strangers, but were often rather lazy in managing their farms and in paying attention to proper crop rotations, even when lairds were trying to control rotations strictly by detailing them under the terms of their leases. They enjoyed going to markets and public places where they could keep in touch with the news of the world, and led a fairly lively social life, sometimes with glass in hand, in the winter months especially. They could be short-tempered, and had a fondness for lawsuits. They were skilled judges of cattle, their main source of income.

A farm group at Craigie Farm bothy, near Leuchars, Fife, in typical attitudes. 1923. Per A. Barron. C10341.

Nickietams, leather straps to keep trouser bottoms up from the mud.
C3083.

The second class consisted of aspiring incomers from the south, said to be intelligent and industrious, and applying agricultural methods far in advance of what was general in the North-East. They dwelt in good houses, which the estates would have recently erected, and lived hospitably and comfortably. They tended to take the lead as incomers are often left to do, in agricultural societies, and in ploughing matches which they liked to organise, and where they acted as judges.

The third group was composed of the younger farmers from the area, no doubt such as would be active in the Scottish Association of Young Farmers' Clubs at the present day. They outdid the incomers — who were not particularly numerous — in enthusiasm and enterprise, and carried the main responsibility for moving along the path of Improvement.

Whatever their nature, the vast majority were tenant farmers, paying their rents to estate factors, and mostly working as much as their men in the fields. They were part of the new farming community, still estate-based, and still requiring the professional services of smith and joiner, but with more coming in from outside and more going out. The new community was part of a much

The lads dressed up in style. Note the hairstyle on the left. At Bethclune, Old Meldrum, Aberdeenshire. C9459.

wider world than the old, and because it had its own kind of organisation, outside views about such organisation, stimulated by the growing social conscience of the nineteenth century, began to impinge on it. However, the new communities remained tightly knit and showed what many would regard as a surprising degree of resistance to outside influence. Even though both married and single men moved with great regularity from farm to farm, they tended to do so within an orbit of ten to twenty miles. They gained a wealth of experience of the land they worked on and of the farmers they worked for. Such movement did not divide the community, but served to create a kind of expanded community or set of overlapping communities whose members had closely shared experiences. There was a sense of brotherhood based on full familiarity with the rhythms and work conventions of their environment.

The firmness of this psychological base, allied to the relatively scattered nature of farm service in comparison with the close associations of workers in factories, meant that attempts to organise men against masters did not make rapid headway. It was not so easy for farm folk to respond to the agitations of industrial workers, though news of these reached them easily enough through the Victorian popular press. Nevertheless, attempts were made to establish societies and unions for farm workers from time to time.

The earliest societies, like the Bell's Wynd Society started in Glasgow in 1746, and the Ploughman's Society established at Cluny Mains in Fife in 1807, were essentially Friendly Societies for the benefit of sick members. They were strictly non-political. They were forms of social insurance rather than means of exerting pressure on employers.

About 1750 a certain 'Windy' Shaw was trying to organise discontented ploughmen in the Carse of Stirling, but without, it seems, any continuing outcome. In 1834, 600 agricultural workers in the Carse of Gowrie formed a union to secure a ten-hour day in summer and an eight-hour day in the winter half-year, with overtime to be paid at day-labourers' rates. Women were active too, for in 1853 those in Sanquhar threatened to stone any shearer who worked for less than 2/6 a day. A short-lived Farm Servants' Union was formed at Dunbar in 1860. A Farm Servants' Protection Society, started in Midlothian in 1865, spread to the rest of the Lothians, Peebles, Berwickshire and Perth, making the basic demands that wages should be 15/- a week, paid fortnightly, with a free house, coal provided and driven at no cost, and a month's food at harvest time.

These efforts in South and Central Scotland ran for a time, and faded out. It was not until the Scottish Farm Servants' Union was founded by Joseph F. Duncan in 1912 that any real degree of continuous progress was made for the whole country. The object of the Union, which spoke of farmworkers as a 'class', was to establish branches throughout Scotland, to consolidate and strengthen the influence and power of farm servants, carters and labourers generally, and to reform and improve relations with employers by getting agreement to monthly payments, indefinite rather than short-term engagements and a weekly half-holiday except during the six busy weeks of harvest. They sought to abolish the bothy system, and to get improvements in food and in accommodation.

In spite of Duncan's efforts, which included the publication from 1913 of a monthly journal, *The Scottish Farm Servant*, it was far through the twentieth century before any degree of solidarity was achieved. The Dumfries branch, for example, ran from 1913 to 1918, and did not take up again till 1935. In 1955, Dumfriesshire

Peeblesshire *bondagers*, female outworkers, at Broughton. Per Mrs. Smith. C4565.

had twenty-one branches, all having to be separately organised.

A curious illustration of the interaction between master and man in the early years of the present century was the 'Turra Coo' incident in Turriff, Aberdeenshire. Following the Liberal Government's National Insurance legislation in 1911, under Lloyd George, there was a widespread feeling of dissatisfaction amongst both farmers and servants, who did not see why they should support, as they saw it, the workers in factories who were far more liable to fall ill, when they themselves were hardly likely to make much use of sickness benefit, thanks to their healthy, open-air life. Accordingly, Robbie Paterson, farmer at Lendrum on the outskirts of Turriff, in agreement with his men, deliberately did not pay the National Insurance quota for them. The outcome was that one of his cows was poinded, and a day set for her sale in the town square, so that the money should be recovered. No one was willing to buy her, and a minor riot followed, at which clods of earth, kail stalks and eggs were thrown at the police and the auctioneer, a man brought in specially from Banff to carry out the sale. The cow escaped, and found her way back to Lendrum.

Shortly after, she was taken by rail to Aberdeen, where a further attempt was made to sell her. This succeeded, not without some difficulty, but later, a number of local farmers clubbed together to buy her back and she was returned to Lendrum after being driven in procession through the town.

The bothie boys at Gagie, Angus, 1906–14. Per Mrs. H. D. McLeisch. C9197.

The incident was a noteworthy example of a genuinely popular reaction to unpopular legislation. There was full reporting in local and even national newspapers. Slogans were created, some of them painted on the cow's sides, local poets and musicians made the most of the occasion, and a children's rhyme appeared:

> Inky poo
> Yer nose is blue
> Ye're aafa like
> The Turra Coo.

Plates, saucers, plaques and engraved glass tumblers recorded the occasion and survive as sought-after items. Modern examples are still being made for sale to Turriff visitors.

Throughout the period of the incident, *The Scottish Farm Servant* continued to make comments. It showed a curious ambivalence. On the one hand it was against the Insurance Act, for various reasons, and on the other it found it hard to support a farmer with such evident business ability as Robbie Paterson. It compromised by treating the Turra Coo and what it stood for as a matter of amusement, which occupied time at Union meetings that would have been better spent on the main issues, which were better

Farmers bought equipment from shops like this in the Grassmarket, Edinburgh. A metal horse-collar, for breaking in young horses, hangs by the door. Left Duncan Robertson; right John Russell, father of A. M. Russell. 1890–1900. Per G. Russell. C18677.

conditions, including recognised, regular breaks, for farm servants.

The incident was important, however. It reflected the characteristic attitudes of the North-East community of the time, and showed without any real room for doubt that there was a great deal of unanimity of feeling between master and men.

This does not mean, of course, that the men were without grievances. On the contrary, they had plenty, but their response lay not in co-ordination of effort through the formalised activities of an established Union, but more through unofficial 'horsemen's societies'. These were strong in the North-East from the nineteenth century until the period when the tractor replaced the horse, between the two World Wars. They did not try to gain their ends, which were often personal in respect of a single specific farmer or his wife, by strikes and walk-outs, but by a discreet use of the 'supernatural'. Clods flying around the house at dead of night, or the sound of an iron-tyred barrow dancing across the close, might have a good effect on a farmer's wife who was providing too monotonous a diet, including oatcakes made thick and green with too much baking soda, or on a farmer who was making working

C

Joseph Duncan, Founder of the Scottish Farm Servants' Union, in his retirement at Newburgh, Aberdeenshire, in 1963. Per I. Carter. C2154.

conditions a bit too harsh.

To become a 'horseman', one of the initiated, it was first necessary for a young lad to have served his apprenticeship on the farm. When he was deemed to be ready to become one of the men, arrangements were made for the horseman ceremony to take place, generally in the barn in the middle of the night. Four established horsemen usually took part. The novice had to bring with him a loaf, a bottle of whisky and a candle. He was blindfolded and led to the 'altar', which could take the shape of a bushel measure pressed on to a sack of corn. He was asked various stock questions to which correct answers had to be given, and then an oath was taken. A version of the oath noted by an Aberdeenshire farm servant who retired to London in 1908 shows that it resembled the Masonic oath. The would-be horseman had to swear never to reveal in any way whatsoever any part of the true horsemanship he was about to receive. In particular it was not be be passed on to any tradesmen, other than those whose work involved horses, nor to a farmer nor a farmer's son, unless he was working his own or his father's horses, nor to any woman. It was not for anyone under the age of 16, nor over 45, by which time, presumably, a horseman was past his prime. The penalty for failing to keep these solemn promises was that 'my flesh be torn to pieces with a wild horse and my heart cut through with a horseman's knife and my bones buried on the sands of the seashore where the tide ebbs and flows every twenty-four hours so that there may be no remembrance of me amongst lawful brethren'.

In conclusion, the novice got a shake of the Devil's hand, a stick covered with a hairy skin, and was then given the Word, of which there were various versions. One was 'Both in one'. By this time, the loaf was no doubt done and the whisky bottle empty.

CHAPTER 8

Homes And Working Places: Traces from The Past

In the days before improvement, buildings in the countryside and on the coasts were strictly functional. Men built them out of the materials that lay at hand — stone and turf and clay and heather — and the most valuable element was the roofing timber. They came out of the environment and in their decay they returned to it, often by way of the middens that fertilised the crops. In this way, the buildings of the old community were themselves part of the energy flow that returned to the land, in one form or another, what was taken from it.

Even at the present day, enough examples survive in corners of the country, on islands and in glens, and scattered here and there in quiet places, to let us get some idea of what small-scale buildings were like in earlier times.

Inside a 'peat-hoose' in Fetlar, Shetland: the late Willie Garriock and Liza Bruce. The fireplace has a stone back, with a wooden 'hangin' lum' to carry off smoke. Photo. I. Petrie, 1920–30. 1.48.7.

In the island of Fetlar in Shetland there is a peninsula called Lambhoga, where people go to cut peat for their fires. It was far enough off to make it necessary to stay there during the periods of work, and at first the only overnight shelter was an old sail. From about the 1860s the idea came of building small houses as more permanent shelters, and thirteen examples remained a hundred years later. They were small, rectangular huts, built of peat from the bog and drift timber from the shore. They had fireplaces with hangin' lums, wooden chimneys fixed against the gables and overhanging the hearth like a canopy, and the only stone in the huts was behind the fireplace, and under it, to prevent the shelter from taking fire.

Some of the hearths had binks or ledges at each side where teapots hottered and pots of herrings and potatoes steamed. A rough wooden table, some stools or benches, and eating utensils, more or less completed the list of furnishings and equipment, except for the most important feature, the bed, which took up a good half of the floor space. It was built of a kind of raised dais of wood and sods, over which heather or straw was spread, then sacking, and the bed was covered with sheets, blankets and a patchwork quilt made of two sewn together to get the necessary width.

It is likely that the inspiration for making these peat-hooses came from the seasonal lodges used by fishermen at remote fishing beaches in other parts of Shetland. In May of each year, from at least the late 1700s, and for as long as the organised hand-fishing of cod, ling and tusk went on, fishermen came to the fishing-stations and re-roofed their lodges with timbers, covering them over with turves, laid to overlap like the scales of a fish to run the water. The walls were of stone, which was plentiful around the beaches, and the lodges were set gable on to the sea, in the manner of old-style fishing-villages everywhere in Scotland. Here, too, half the floor space was given over to the bed in which the fishing-boat crew could rest.

These simple structures represent a much older tradition of dwellings used for seasonal purposes, the most widespread of which was the shieling hut. Most shieling huts were in groups, matching the parent village at a lower level, and sited near streams or lochs, convenient for water and trout. The more recent nineteenth-century examples are rectangular in shape like the

Shetland fishermen's lodges and the peat-houses, but the older ones are round or oval in shape. Surviving examples are built of turf and stone. There is no doubt, however, that slighter materials were once fairly common, as in an eighteenth-century drawing of shieling huts in the island of Jura. These were of branches or wattle like big Indian wigwams, and covered over with turf to keep the insides dry. Once such flimsy structures decayed, little trace of them would remain.

Many good examples of stone and turf 'beehive' huts remain in the hills of Lewis. The lower courses, up to a height of 3ft., were built of double walls of stone totalling about 6ft. thick. Above this level the walls were single. Each course oversailed the one below, becoming narrower all the time, till they drew in at the top, at a height of 8 or 9ft., to leave a round opening which acted as a smoke outlet when the door was shut. No timbers were needed in such a construction. Inside, they measured about 7 or 8ft. across by about 6 or 7ft. high. Quite often, even in the smallest huts, there were two little doors, one or the other of which was used according to the lie of the wind. The fire was lit between the doors in a shallow wall recess, at floor level, since peat, unlike coal, has no need of an air-space below to provide a draught. In the walls were recesses for the milk vessels and other items. Again, much of the floor area was given over to the bed-space, often bounded at the front by a low wall of stones topped with turf, which also served as a seat before the fire.

Many shieling huts had a smaller one close to or attached to them, as a store for milking equipment, milk and cheese, for a few creelfuls of seaweed carried up from the shore (where accessible) as a tasty bite for the cows during milking, and as a shelter for new-born calves.

Such beehive huts were by no means confined to Lewis. Their foundations have been surveyed in Sutherland, in Perthshire and in the Glens of Angus. In general, the form was dying out in the late eighteenth century when newer, bigger rectangular huts began to be built, themselves a sign of changing times in the shieling grounds. The stone-built oval huts, however, with their egg-shaped roofs, are similar to structures in several countries that may go back to prehistoric times. They mark a very ancient and very widespread building tradition, whilst, on the other hand, the rectangular buildings that replaced them are in line with the

A gable of alternating stone and turf, on a house in the township of Skerray on the north coast of Sutherland. AF, 1985. 53.14.41.

strong thrust of the improvement spirit that pervaded every aspect of life from around the 1770s.

Change can be seen in permanently occupied buildings too. It does not always follow that improvements bring universal benefits in their train. Those who were forced to the edges of the improved farms, or small tradesmen who provided necessary services, did not have houses put up for them by the estates. They had to do the best they could with the resources available to them, and in doing so, sometimes carried on much older techniques.

An example of this is a way of building in alternate courses of stone and turf. Where there were only round and pebbly stones that were of little use for making a wall by themselves, the system was to lay a course of stones, then a double course of turf, then stones, and so on to the top, using the turf as a kind of sandwich-filling to give the stones cohesion. The technique is known in historical sources from the early 1600s, but in the later 1700s and into the 1800s there was a spread in its use, especially in the Borders and around the Grampians.

It was possible, it seems, to rickle up a house in a day, if the turf and stones had been brought together first. In the Borders, cottars' and shepherds' houses, about 12ft. square and with walls 5ft. high,

The smithy at Greenscares, Gamrie, Banffshire, built of stone and with a gable of clay. Per J. H. Littlejohn. C7164.

were built like this. The same technique was used in the Grampians for the houses of weavers and other tradesmen, which were rapidly knocked up on allotments of waste land.

In these cases, the dwellings were of a relatively short-term nature, though by no means seasonal. In the higher parts of Banff and Moray, however, in Angus, and across to the isle of Arran in the west, crofts and even farmhouses and steadings were built in alternating stone and turf, as was a church at Achadh na h-uaidh in Sutherland.

When a technique is used by a range of social strata in such a way it can safely be assumed that it is quite old. In fact, the foundations of excavated Viking houses in the North and West of Scotland were sometimes built in the same way. The technique is very likely to have survived between the Viking period and the first historical evidence of 1629. It has, indeed, continued till the present day, for examples of such walling have turned up in both internal and external gables in Sutherland; in Angus at Glenesk, Kirriemuir and Murroes; and in Perthshire at Rait village, Kilspindie.

Alternating stone and turf is arranged in horizontal courses. These two media could also be combined vertically, especially in dwellings of a more substantial nature. There are at least two major systems.

The first is that the lower part of the wall of a house could be of stone and the upper part of turf. Walls could, of course, be entirely of turf, but unless this was very thick, the footings would get damp and the wall would not have long-term stability. Turf walls, even if on a stone base, still did not have the load-bearing ability to take a heavy roof. They had to be assisted, therefore, by the insertion of a special kind of roofing timber known as a cruck-couple, the main feature of which was that the couple legs did not stop at eaves' height, but ran right down more or less to floor level. Theoretically, it was possible to set up the timbers, put on the sods and thatch to cover the roof, and fill in the walls afterwards.

With the possible exception of the islands, cruck-couples seem to have been widespread throughout the country. This in turn suggests that an enormous amount of turf was formerly used in walling. The point is emphasised by the fact that the roofing timbers were held to be the most valuable part of the house. From Caithness to Galloway, it was as a rule the laird's job to provide roofing timbers, which were called the master wood, master's timbers or great timber, whilst the tenant himself saw to the roof-covering and walls. A tenant who moved might take his roof timbers with him, and this clearly worried some lairds, for on the estate of Barclay of Urie in Kincardineshire in 1701, tenants were being forbidden to take down any more of the house walls than was necessary to get the timbers out. In this case the timbers seem to have belonged to the tenants. In the 1760s in Inverness-shire, some lairds were beginning to doubt the wisdom of letting tenants have roofing timber, which must have been cruck-couples, because it led to sub-standard walls, and Mr Grant of the Seafield estate actually stopped giving his tenants timber for their side walls. As a result, they were forced to build their walls of stone. Modern times, and the end of cruck-couples, were on their way, though in fact crucks continued to be used along with stone walls for some time to come. Since most stone walls were fully load-bearing in any case, the combination was really an anachronism, a pointer to a technique so ingrained in the traditional knowledge of the people that it could not be easily discarded.

The second vertical form of stone and turf combination belongs to North-West Scotland, including the Hebrides. It goes with the so-called blackhouse, a type of building unique in Britain, with a double wall, in the centre of which is an infill of turf. The old

The old blackhouses at the farming village of Arnol in Lewis, with modern houses alongside. AF, 1973. 53.14.45.

beehive shieling huts were also partly built in this technique. Most travellers who see blackhouses for the first time are impressed with their primitive appearance. The roof rests on the inside half of the wall and the top of the outer half forms a ledge, along which a man can walk, and sometimes adventurous sheep also. Some had chimneys or smoke-openings, and some had none. Window spaces were few and far between.

Yet, as they exist now, for example the one preserved by the Scottish Development Department at 42 Arnol in Lewis, they are 'improved' versions of older forms, which modern ideas and ideals began to affect nearly a century after the main thrust of housing improvement had passed in Lowland Scotland. When the officers of the Ordnance Survey were touring these areas about 1850, taking notes in preparation for making the maps of the country, they frequently added comments about what they saw around them. From this source, it is evident that at that date, only the inner skins of the blackhouses were of stone, to take the weight of the roof. The outside was simply a thick layer of turf, such as can also be seen on some of the surviving shieling huts. The adoption of the outer skin of stone, therefore, is a form of upgrading, which replaced an even greater earlier use of turf, laid vertically, in such houses.

Another important building material was clay. It was used not only in the countryside, but in towns also. There were clay houses in Forres in 1586, in Tain in the 1780s (these were two-storey examples), in nineteenth-century Garmouth in Moray, in the weaving village of Luthermuir in Angus that was founded in 1828, and in the Perthshire town of Errol, where substantial clay-walled houses still remain, though the clay is harled over.

The tradition was old in towns where the raw material could be got. What was new was its late eighteenth and nineteenth-century spread into the countryside, from Ross down the east coast and across to Wigton. Clay was dug from pits, and thoroughly mixed with chopped straw, heather or other fibrous material, or small gravelly stones. It was usually laid in courses about 2½ft. deep, each of which was allowed to harden before the next went on.

In such details of buildings, pointers can be got to the appearance of the houses people lived in before the period of massive change brought about by the improvements, and to continuing aspects of older traditions for the houses of the less well-off. In any country community, houses had walls of stone and much turf, roofing couples with legs that came to floor level, and roof-coverings of spars and branches, turves and thatch.

They were not necessarily arranged neatly in lines or squares, but what was almost invariable was a close and intimate relationship between the byre and the living space under one roof. The milking of cows, feeding of calves, and processing of milk has always been women's work, and it is hardly surprising that throughout Scotland, as in many other countries, cows, young stock and people lived under the same ridge-pole. Several examples of such 'long houses' have survived in the remoter parts of Scotland, including Shetland, Orkney and Caithness, and in the west the blackhouse with its double walls is a special variety, but all were swept away in the Lowlands as improvements advanced. There is no doubt, however, that the form was once quite general, and lay so deep in the minds of the country dwellers that efforts made by lairds to make them change were sometimes strongly resisted. In Lewis, for example, Lord Seaforth was instructing his tenants in the 1830s to put up partitions between themselves and their cattle, and to let more light into their houses. He succeeded only in part, 'sorely against the wishes of the people'. In 1872, crofters in the township of Barvas were made to improve their

The Midlothian village of Swanston, on the edge of Edinburgh, before being modernised and thatched with reeds. AF, 1957. 53.14.47.

houses by putting in two doors and making a division between house and byre, the proprietor himself supplying doors, windows and woodwork. Still in 1886 there were complaints about 'the obstinate retention of cattle under the roof', and in 1893, the Lewis District Commission was instructing the Sanitary Inspector to take legal proceedings where necessary. Yet as recently as 1947, about 40% of the Lewis homesteads still had house and byre under one roof, with internal communication between. This situation is an outstanding example of how difficult it can be to erode or erase the built-in attitudes of centuries.

CHAPTER 9

The Great Rebuild

The intensity of the agricultural improvements in Lowland Scotland meant that the past was almost totally swept away, including the old ferm-touns, the little farming villages. As part and parcel of the enclosure movement and the making of individual farms, went the building of new accommodation.

The first writer to talk about the layout of farm-buildings in any detail was Lord Belhaven in 1699, though he seems to have been making proposals rather than outlining an existing situation. He said that the dwelling-house, the 'sit-house', should lie east and west, with south-facing windows to catch the sun.

The barns should lie at the west end of the house, lying north-south. This meant that their two opposite doors could catch the prevailing east-west winds, so that corn could be winnowed more effectively. He recommended three barns, one for wheat and barley, one for oats and one for pease, although this, of course, points to

A new-style Kincardineshire farm in 1813. House and garden are a little aside from the steading. The cottar house, thatched and not slated, stands clear of the farm. From G. Robertson, *Agriculture of Kincardine*, 1813. C673.

71

the relatively big-scale farming of East Lothian. West of the barns should be the stackyard, preferably on a piece of rising ground to catch the wind and help the corn in the stacks to dry.

The stables and byres should not be alongside the house but at the opposite side of the close, with their doors facing the house for readier access. The east side of the close should contain the chaff-house, and the entrance to the close should lie between it and the house, at the cleanest possible position, above the dunghill which occupied the middle.

Belhaven recommended that the walls of the house, at least, should be of stone and lime. Clay or earth was no doubt the common mortar of the period, and remained so for smaller farms and cottages well into the nineteenth century. He still spoke of turf and plenty of straw thatch as the preferred roofing medium. A century was to pass before slates and clay pantiles became common.

Belhaven was concerned not only with the buildings themselves, but also with their surrounds. Yards or gardens should be planted with ash and elm trees, to be used eventually for the upkeep of the house. The garden plants were to include cabbage and kail, potatoes and turnips, and a few 'Turkie beans' or ordinary beans and peas to go with pork. It is curious that he does not mention rhubarb, so prevalent at least in later times. He does mention leeks and chives as items for the tables of gentlefolk only.

This seventeenth-century description of a farmhouse and steading built round four sides of a square was, for its time, a forward-looking scheme. There was as yet no suggestion that the dunghill should not be in the middle of the close, nor that the dwelling-house should be more separate from the steading. This degree of sophistication, often with a clump of trees as a screen between house and steading, was to come on big farms some generations later. By the late nineteenth century it had spread right down the farming ladder to include even units of under 100 acres.

Generally speaking, it appears that building improvements began in the main grain-growing areas, and in areas where stock-rearing was active, both of these criteria coinciding with forward-looking lairds. In fact, Belhaven's ideas were to some extent foreshadowed in 1649, at West Gagie in Angus, where the house and some of the offices were on three sides of a square. These offices, however, probably concerned domestic activities, for the

The farm of Horn, Angus. The two-storey farm-house is built of clay.
AF, 1973. 53.14.37.

four byres, stable, three barns and henhouse of this substantial
farm formed a second group, possibly around a second yard. In
1705, the factor for the Earl of Panmure at Belhelvie in
Aberdeenshire had a substantial house to which were attached one
or more one-storey ranges of outbuildings, including three barns
and four byres. Their arrangement is not known. In 1717, Over
Moss-houses in Midlothian, on the Clerk of Penicuik estate, had a
house flanked by two service wings, and the fourth side was also
closed, possibly by a wall.

These points show that Belhaven was simply crystallising in
print ideas and practices that were very much in the air, possibly
stemming from the laird's house and its courtyard of offices.
However, the real period of new building that went hand-in-hand
with the period of widespread agricultural improvement began in
the 1760s-70s. What Belhaven's description came to look like on
the ground can be seen from a description of a Midlothian mains
farm in 1793. A set of low buildings formed a square, one side of
which was the house. It had two or three rooms floored with earth,
low ceilings, and a few small windows. A cruck-framed barn with
side-walls 5ft. high took up another side. Opposite it were the byre
and stables. The stables were not divided into stalls, and the horses

A small, late eighteenth century Angus farm, south of Glamis, partly slated and partly roofed with clay-impregnated reeds. AF, 1975. 53.14.31.

were kept, and fed, loose inside. The byre had no wooden stalls either, but the head of each animal was fixed to an upright stake. Byre fittings of this type survived in West Lothian and Peeblesshire almost till the present time. This Midlothian farm unit, however, was smaller than what Belhaven had in mind, and it also included servants' cottages on the fourth side of the square.

By the 1790s, a unit like this was already being thought of as old-style. From surveys made in the 1760s-70s, an impression can be got of the rate of the great rebuild that was going on, and it is clear also that many of the new farms and steadings were rising on former outfield areas. Division of former commonties between proprietors aided the spread of farms, and had at the same time a considerable influence on building materials. People used to getting turf and divots from the moor for walling and roofing purposes could no longer get these resources so readily. The alternatives were the more costly walls of stone and roofs of slates and tiles. It may be that lairds were more or less obliged to make an investment in forms of housing superior to what had been needed in the past, on behalf of their new-day tenants, from whom they expected to get rents at a level high enough to produce returns on

A house at Cranloch, Llanbryde, Morayshire, newly thatched by John Brockie, using a clay and straw mixture. AF, 1966. 53.14.33.

their investment. It is significant that this estate investment was countrywide for all the farming areas, and, with a century's delay, in the crofting areas. This is in itself an acknowledgement of the important role that the resources of the outfield and commons had in pre-improvement days. Without them, input from the estates was needed to get the new-style farming on to its feet.

As commons were reclaimed and the old outfield was broken in for what were called 'centrical' or individual enclosed farms, and as the old joint-farming communities were phased out, building activity was intense. Not only farms, but also buildings in villages were in a state of rapid expansion. This was, of course, an important means of absorbing people displaced from the countryside. As an example, Simprin in Berwickshire grew from a population of 100 in 1770 to 351 in 1793. Growth did not go along with poorer living conditions, but just the opposite, for by the latter date, every house had a clock, many of the people carried watches, and as well as eating home-made oatcakes, they were buying loaf bread brought from the surrounding towns: Edinburgh, Berwick, Duns, Coldstream and Norham. Proximity to Northumberland no doubt gave Simprin an advantage, however, and improvements in living standards were slower in other areas, but at least the general direction of movement was set.

Simprin is an example of expansion of an existing village. Many new ones were founded by lairds, like Castletown in Roxburgh. It was built by the Duke of Buccleuch on the farm of Park, with two streets at right angles, a central square and two smaller squares. It was started in 1793 and by 1795 had twenty-three houses, each with two acres of ground, enough to make an incoming countryman feel that he had not been too much divorced from his roots.

All of these activities gave a boost to a variety of trades. Thatchers, though continuing to have outlets for their skills, began to give way to slaters and tradesmen skilled in applying roofing tiles. Quarries for good building stone and for dykes flourished, and quarriers, stonemasons and dykers were in full demand. Such men were a further essential element in the infrastructure of services that changing times demanded.

It is a general truism that improvements in accommodation for the farmer and his family, and for the farm produce and stock, came first, to be followed only after a long gap by that for farm workers. Farmworker housing did exist earlier, though it was not of great quality. A traveller through East Lothian in 1661 observed that servants lived in 'pitiful Cots', built of stone and covered with turf, one-roomed, often without chimneys and with small, unglazed window openings. By the sixteenth century, 'cot-house' or 'cottar house' were names clearly used for farmworkers' housing, either singly, or in groups to which the term 'cot-town', still a common place-name, was applied. The groups could be of four or more, clustered, or in a row near the farm-steading. For the most part, those living in cot-houses were married. Single men and women servants lived and were boarded in the households of the farmers.

The Midlothian workers' cottages at the side of the square of the mains farm described in 1793 were probably about 12ft. square. Alexander Somerville, who published his *Autobiography of a Working Man* in 1848, described how he was brought up in such a place in Berwickshire. The living space was about 12 x 14ft., and not quite high enough at the sides for a man to stand upright. There was a clay floor, and no ceiling. Internal divisions were made by the beds. The grate was made of iron bars the tenants brought with them, and took away again when they left. Even the window of four small, fixed panes was carried by tenants from house to house.

A double farm-servants' house in 1795 in Midlothian. From G. Robertson, *Agriculture of Midlothian*, 1795. C3924.

In the better farming districts, some improvement was beginning by the 1790s. In Midlothian, some of the new homes were bigger, 16 to 18ft., with good mason-work walls 7 to 8ft. high. The roofs were of neat straw thatch, and some were ceiled, and had timber floors. The question of siting also came into play. No longer were they built near the midden, but at a distance from the farmhouse, perhaps a hundred yards away or so. There were often several in a row, continuing a tradition that had started with the older cot-houses.

Farther north in Fife, in isolated pockets, new housing was comparable though on a slightly smaller scale. Just before 1800, sizes of 15-16ft. with stone-and-lime side walls 6-7ft. high, are mentioned, in units of three or four to eight or ten houses. These could be let not only to married servants, but also to tradesmen or labourers during the hay and grain harvests and other busy seasons. They were built, it seems, with a shrewd eye to farming as a business.

By the 1860s there were major improvements, and rebuilding of farmworker housing was widespread. In 1832, the Highland and Agricultural Society of Scotland was offering premiums for essays on the construction of improved dwellings. The Society also

The *chaumer* at Brownhill, Auchterless, Aberdeenshire, built 1902. AF, 1983. 53.14.27.

encouraged well-kept gardens. These factors, plus pressures from the kirk against the immorality of large families in single-room dwellings, led to the building of two and three-roomed houses. The basic elements were a kitchen-cum-living-cum-sleeping room, a bedroom, and a kind of larder for dairy produce and household necessities. It is a curious aspect of national differences that whereas English farmworkers liked an upstairs bedroom, in Scotland there was a general preference for one-storey houses. This changed in the latter part of the nineteenth century. Now most existing farmworkers' houses are on two floors.

Improvement in the actual building was not always accompanied by better facilities. An outside dry-closet, an ash-pit at the back, and water to be carried some distance from a well are features still well within living memory. The pages of *The Scottish Farm Servant* were full of denunciation of lairds. In 1913, one writer said: 'I have heard of an old but-and-ben which was "improved" by heightening of the roof and slating it, and into the gable of which the coat of arms of the Duke who owned the property was placed, but for which no water supply was provided, and no privy erected'. Even in the advanced Lothians, some one-roomed houses, usually roofed with tiles, were still to be found at this period. One of the reasons why improvement was so patchy — and it has to be remembered that though farmworker housing was given publicity, the same deficiencies applied to crofts and small farms also — was that farmworkers, married or single, moved very frequently, and in a sense all their homes were temporary. There was little incentive for the occupants to look after them, nor for the owners to fit them out beautifully for occupants who were likely to be careless with them.

Besides such cottar-houses for married servants and their families, there was also accommodation for the unmarried workers, in bothies or in chaumers.

Bothies seem to have begun in Angus and the Mearns in the late 1700s, and then spread to parts of Fife, the Lothians, Berwickshire, the eastern parts of Ross and Cromarty, and Caithness. They mark the major farming areas. Most were for men, but some, as near as Dundee and in Caithness, were for women workers, many of whom were seasonal immigrants from Ireland, or from the Highlands.

Chaumers were to be found on the medium-sized farms in West-Central, but mainly in North-East Scotland. They were furnished as for bothies, with built-in wooden beds and chaff-filled mattresses, and the men's kists in which they kept their belongings. The main difference was that in the bothies the occupants made their own food, whilst the 'chaumer boys' were fed in the kitchen of the farm.

The geographical spread of cottar-houses, bothies and chaumers has varied a good deal from time to time, partly as a result of changing preferences for male or female workers. In an article in the farming paper, *The North British Agriculturist*, in 1852, Mr Cowie of Halkerton Mains in Angus said that most proprietors and farmers were removing old cottar-houses or leaving them to fall down, without replacing them. This made it difficult to house married men, and the bothy became the standard unit of housing in the district.

By the 1860s, nearly every lowland farm in Angus and Kincardineshire had a bothy. Aberdeenshire had a few on larger farms after the 1830s, and by 1849 about 5% of the Aberdeenshire labour force, i.e. about 520 men, were bothied. Bothies then fell in numbers, and by the First World War none seems to have survived. It was very much the same in Banffshire.

These two counties were basically chaumer areas. In Moray and

The double cottar house of Midtown of Pitglassie, Auchterless, Aberdeenshire, (above) as it was, with the ash-pit at the back and no running water, (below) made into a single home, harled and with a heightened roof. AF, 1960s and 1981. 8.21.8, 7A; 53.14.23.

Nairn this was also true, though change took another direction after 1860, when a movement of farm servants from Ross-shire brought with them the custom of living in bothies, to such an extent that by the 1880s they were the main form of servant housing on most farms. From the 1890s, however, bothies began to fade out in Nairn, leaving chaumers supreme for housing single men.

These variations show the changing fortunes of farming in different regions, different scales of farming and differences in the attitudes of farmers to the kind of workforce they preferred, always with an eye to keeping wages at a minimum.

Leaving aside the social background, however, a general point can be made in relation to the great rebuild, which got into its stride in the 1770s and was still being followed out in the 1900s with farm-servant housing. Improvements to crofts and small farms could be even more recent. For the most part, the rebuild was estate-inspired. It was based on architectural theory and practice, and on pattern books for estate buildings. It includes the but-and-ben type cottage, widely held in much affection, and all the estate buildings, gardeners' cottages and the like, which can still be readily seen on journeys through Scotland. Outside the immediate 'big hoose' precincts are the farmhouses, outhouses, and servants' housing, and the smithies and joiners' shops, all more or less conforming to the architectural principles of the great rebuild. It is little wonder, therefore, that there is a high degree of uniformity in overall proportions, in the relationship of door and window openings and porches to the façade as a whole. This applies at almost all social levels regardless of size. The outcome is that through much of Scotland there is an appearance of similarity about these buildings, most of which date from some period during the last 200 years. It is a modernised building landscape. In its uniformity it conceals what was originally a much more varied and in some ways sophisticated tradition of building, a tradition using stone, turf, clay, wood and wattle separately and in combination, in conformity with ways of building established by centuries of application, and much more in line with wider European traditions. What we have gained in physical comfort, we have lost in terms of contact with that tradition. Nevertheless, scattered traces of that remoter past are still with us, and it is a fascinating piece of detective work to find them out.

CHAPTER 10

The Peat Fire Flame

The fire was the most important part of a home, around which people have gathered for food and warmth from the beginnings of time. By day it was the woman's domain. At night, the family gathered there. The gathering and storing of fuel for it was an inescapable part of the daily and seasonal rhythm.

Peat was the main source of fuel for centuries. Even yet about 10% of Scotland's land surface is peat-bog, and peat is still in use as fuel, and for gardens. Peat goes with the tradition of the open hearth at floor level. It was the open hearth that characterised the form of the fireplace until well through the nineteenth century, and in places it is surviving still.

Amongst the poorest levels of society, regular heating was one of the last things to be thought of. A temporary fire of poor quality or of very quick-burning fuel was often the best they could manage for basic cooking or for heating liquids. Energy spent in gathering

A back-burden of brushwood for the fire, at Bracora, Morar. Per Mrs J. Telfer Dunbar. C18397.

fuel was often scarcely returned in terms of heat. This must have been true from prehistoric times till the heyday of the welfare state. Eighteenth and nineteenth-century sources tell that fires were hardly kindled at all in the homes of poor folk, except for cooking victuals. Distress in severe winters was 'unspeakably great', and the daylight hours of women and children were often spent in gathering firing, such as bits of brushwood, whins and broom, or heather, to get some scanty heat in the evenings.

There was so much dependence on peat for fuel in general that all classes of the country community were forced to look for alternatives in districts where peat had been worked out.

Turf was one possibility, though under the old community organisation extensive use of turf for fuel could seriously interfere with the grazing. The regulations of local Baron Courts tried to prevent this abuse of resources. In 1604, for example, the Earl of Erroll forbade tenants in Urie, Kincardineshire, to supply the inhabitants of Stonehaven with peat, turf or heather for fuel, and made the farmers answerable for their servants. Frequent repetition of the regulations over the next century and a half suggests that they were not conspicuously successful.

It is not easy now to imagine the enormous amounts of turf cut by the flauchter or turf spade, for all the conceivable purposes of the old community. Each farming settlement would have been surrounded by stretches of bare ground, marked by the scoop-like hollows left by the flauchter spade. An extreme example is the present-day appearance of the island of Papa Stour in Shetland, where the two-thirds of the land surface lying outside the township dyke have been lifted and transported on to the remaining third after centuries of intensive utilisation. As a kind of standard sequence of change due to the search for fuel, peat supplies were first used up, then turf was cut to burn at the expense of grazing, or some other fuel had to be found.

One such was dried animal manure, sometimes used by the poor in parts of mainland Scotland, for example in Galloway, and in Fife and Angus where coal-dross or sawdust was mixed with dung and made into large cakes to be dried in the sun. In island areas, however, where peat and turf were scarce or non-existent — North Ronaldsay and Sanday in Orkney, and in Heiskir, Muck, Tiree and Canna in the Hebrides — dried horse- or cow-dung, eked out by seaweed, was widely burned.

(Left) Will Strachan cutting peat at the Crombie Moss, Banffshire. AF, 1968. 53.10.20. (Right) Wheeling the peats on the peat barrow to be laid out flat to dry. AF, 1968. 53.10.23.

Peat, however, was the sought-after fuel, doubly important as long as there was a tax on coal. This tax was lifted in 1793. What differentiated peat from the foraging for short-term fuels that marked the struggles of poorer folk was the need for organisation in cutting, drying and transporting, sometimes for long distances, and then stacking near the houses for convenient use. People were prepared to go long distances by land and sea for their essential supply.

The techniques of cutting peat varied from place to place, like the shapes of the spades used to cut it. The first job was to open the peat bank by clearing the heather top layer to get at the softer fuel below, by using an ordinary spade of the gardening variety, or a flauchter spade, separately or with a special knife to slice through tough roots. Peat was cut with an eye to conservation of resources, and the regulations of estates, which usually owned and allocated the peat banks, showed an awareness of the need to do so. The top surface was laid with reasonable care at the bottom of the bank, so that it should form what would soon be a possible grazing surface again. It also had the immediate practical benefit of providing a surface to stand on, where cutting was done into the face of the bank rather than down from the top.

The types of spades and the techniques of cutting were much influenced by the nature of the peat itself. In most extensive blanket peat bogs where the peat was a solid mass of decayed sphagnum and heather and plant roots the usual method was from the top. One man cut and an assistant caught a peat off the spade, and laid it on top of the bank for the first stage of drying, but Shetland had a different method. The custom was for one man to cut with his light peat spade, the tusker, and swing the peat up on

(Left) The second drying stage is to raise the peats into little heaps. AF, 1968. 53.10.2. (Right) Having a piece to eat at the break. AF, 53.10.24.

to the bank, on the blade, by himself. In areas where the peat took the form of narrow stratified layers, formed by deposits of bog-bean and weeds in the beds of ancient lakes, cutting had to be in from the face, and the spade-blade was broader. This helped to keep the peats whole in longitudinal layers during drying. Cutting from the top would have led to flaking into a large number of little slices that would have separated like leaf tobacco. There are at least a dozen varieties of peat-spades that can be related to the different regions of Scotland. The ecological ties between the nature of the deposit, the instrument used, and the work team, were very close.

Everyone helped at peat-cutting, friends and neighbours together. Food for the group could be prepared in the open on a peat fire, with potatoes boiled in their skins and water for tea boiled in a thick, cast-iron kettle. All around on a fine day was the buzzing of insects, loudest when there was no wind to wipe away sweat, and the shimmer of sun over the glistening black lines of the opened banks, with the houses of the township below, and the sea beyond. Peat work is one of the community tasks that is also a pleasure. It has survived from the dim days of the past, and in peat-rich areas the smell of peat-reek still scents the air.

The amount of peat needed for a year's firing can come as a surprise. Fifty or sixty loads would keep one fire going for a year, and the cutting, drying and carting of this quantity would take a full month of a man's time, though in practice he would not do this alone. When stacked up around the houses of a township, the peat

The peats are home and stacked for winter fires. AF, 1968. 53.10.22.

stacks could almost dwarf the buildings. To see this sight is to realise the enormous areas of peat that have been cleared through centuries, and some understanding can be gained of how immense the change in the appearance of the landscape is. In Lowland Scotland, peat has been mostly used up, and all that remains is the flatness of original bogs, now fields, that bear crops or graze farming stock. The wide selection of peat-spades from all parts of Scotland, now mostly preserved in museums, is the only other surviving physical evidence of the annual task of fuel getting.

Peat burned in an open hearth gave energy as heat, and also as fertiliser, for the ashes were returned to the fields directly or by way of the byre where they served to soak up urine in the bedding. It had the advantage over coal that it had no need for a draught of air underneath. Open, peat-fired hearths were always at floor level, otherwise they would burn out too quickly and would not stay alight overnight, as they were usually expected to do. Such hearths in the old farming communities could be found in a surprising variety of forms.

Of these, the central hearth was the simplest. Examples survive in the North and West, for example at 42 Arnol in Lewis. The central fire on a circle or square of flat stones, usually set in clay, goes back to prehistoric times. Sometimes there was no chimney,

A pony with creels of-peat in the island of Eigg. M. E. M. Donaldson, about 1910. 51.18.29.

and the smoke simply filled the space and oozed out through the door, at the eaves, or where it could; or else there was a smoke-opening in the ridge of the roof, through which a good deal of the smoke could escape. In a house with no chimney, anyone standing upright would find the smoke annoying. The important thing was to sit down as quickly as possible, since the spreading heat from the fire kept the smoke above the level of the sitters' heads. Though the survival area is the North and West, it has to be realised that central hearths were once common everywhere. The artist Joseph Farrington drew one, for example, in 1792, in a house built of turf in the Carse of Stirling.

The first form of sophistication was in the addition of a backing stone or part wall between the hearth and the door. Stone backs are known in Orkney and Caithness, and one was excavated in a late eighteenth-century house at Lix in Central Perthshire, where the byre lay immediately behind the backing stone. The Caithnesians called this stone the brace or brace-steen. It was said to divide the room into 'fore 'e fire' (before the fire), where the family sat, and 'back o' the fire', where barrels, tubs, peats, etc., were stored. The use of such stones seems to date to the early beginnings of Improvement, and marks the relatively new concept of a more formal division of space in the kitchen area, one part for day-to-day living, and one for stores and lumber.

As modern times came nearer, this division was emphasised by extending the back to make a cross-wall, so that two rooms appeared where one had been before, or else the fireplace was moved to a gable. In each case, the effect was to produce a gable fireplace. These varied greatly in type, especially in the nature of the chimney arrangement, although the position of the fire at floor level remained the same at first.

Movement of the central hearth to the gable, as the kitchen fireplace, was a mark of social change in itself. It also coincided with the adoption of fireplaces in best rooms. Such rooms began to appear in croft and smaller farm houses as units separate from those where the everyday business of living went on. They were reserved for solemn and festive times, and for visitors of prestige like the minister.

The best room and kitchen ends not only had these differences in function, but also had different forms of hearth. It was in the best rooms that coal-burning grates began to be fitted, matched by chimneys in the thickness of the gable wall, even if coal was too costly to use much. It was all very well for a large mansion house with large numbers of servants to have coal fires in every room, including the master's and mistress's bedrooms and dressing-rooms, but lesser folk had to be more sparing. In Wigtown, by 1795, the 'better class' of inhabitants were using coal in their rooms, though peat remained the kitchen fuel. It was said that the growth

A central hearth, with a peat-fire burning, in a blackhouse at Calbost, Lewis. AF, 1964. 53.14.79.

of the spinning industry about the same date in Dyke and Moy, Moray, encouraged the people to start using coal early, since it gave enough light for them to see to work in the evening. The use of grates developed first near coal-bearing areas, however, and then around ports and landing places for the seaborne coal trade. Whenever coal was the fuel, raised grates were needed to get the necessary draught, as the people of Forglen in Banffshire found in 1795. They had been trying coal on their floor-level kitchen fires, without outstanding success. Scarcity of peat also, of course, encouraged quicker adoption of coal and grates, and in some areas only a few loads of peat were got to serve as kindling when lighting a coal fire. Not only built-in grates were used, however, but also free-standing braziers, some of which had an ash-hole underneath. Coal-burning, therefore, had an entirely practical function where coal was freely available and where there was a special need for it, and a prestige function elsewhere by the end of the eighteenth century. Nevertheless the peat-fired kitchen hearth did not pass away then, nor is it dead yet.

Change in the kitchen hearth also marked social progress with special regard to smoke extraction. Chimneys in the thickness of the gable became standard in best rooms in the late eighteenth and nineteenth centuries, but only in the late nineteenth and early twentieth centuries in kitchens. Gable chimneys had reached as far north as Shetland by the early 1800s, and were fairly common by the 1830s. Caithness had some improved cottages with a chimney in one room by 1812, although this innovation was still rare in the county in the 1840s. In the North-East, best-room fires with gable chimneys were burning for special occasions by the 1790s. Farther south, however, gable chimneys for the two main rooms of houses were much more common. When coal was easy to get, it was cheaper than peat, because of the time and effort needed to process peat.

One of the earliest means of improving smoke-extraction was to build a hangin' lum, or canopy chimney, over the hearth. When a new farmhouse was built near Balquhidder in Perthshire in 1771, with a stair and a loft and four windows with glass panes, the kitchen was fitted with a 'Lothian brace' costing 5/-. The name of this wooden hood points to Lothian as an innovation area, and in fact a mid-nineteenth-century manuscript describes such a fireplace in the Lothians as 'a grate of a particular form set up against the gavel projecting all its width from the wall, two timber pillars at the corners supporting the timber lum which ascends about three feet from the fire-place. The reik does not ascend through a vent within the end wall or gable but through a timber frame connected with this brace and set up against the gavel'.

This was without doubt a form of gable hood. The South-East also produced an alternative solution to smoke removal, without moving the hearth from a central position in the room. What was called in 1802 the 'round-about fire side' was in wide use in Peeblesshire kitchens. It was 'a circular grate placed upon the floor about the middle of the kitchen, with a frame of lath and plaster, or spars and mats, suspended over it ... like an inverted funnel, for conveying the smoke; the whole family sitting around the fire within the circumference of the inverted funnel'. This same device, an inverted canopy slung from the ceiling and not set against the gable, also characterised Roxburgh and Selkirkshire. It was on quite a big scale, for it formed a unit, almost a room within a room, capable of seating the family around the fire in the evenings.

The 'Lothian brace' was probably not as large, but a mid-

A central hearth with a backstone, excavated in a late eighteenth or early nineteenth century house at Lix, Perthshire. The byre was just beyond the backstone. The entrance door to the house led through the byre. AF, 1961. 53.14.17.

nineteenth-century version in Lanarkshire was so arranged that there was room for a wooden settle for the young farm lads in the 6ft. space between the fire and the gable wall, under a hood about 5-6ft. wide, placed about 6ft. above the fire, and contracting to 2ft. square. At the top, by this date, it could be carried into a part chimney built in the thickness of the upper part of the gable, or else the hood was carried through the ridge, near the gable, in the form of a box that projected 3ft. and was wound around with straw ropes.

Alongside such improvements there were occasional survivals of older systems. For example, a rare photograph of the farm of Eastfield, Lanarkshire, taken in the later nineteenth century, shows a large kitchen with a flagstone floor. Against one wall is a large 'swey' or crane, made of wood, for hanging pots above the fire. The fire, seemingly of coal, is set in an elongated iron brazier standing on four legs above an open ash-pit, well out towards the middle of the floor. There is no trace of a chimney hood.

In spite of such survivals, there is little doubt that in the Lothians and adjacent Border counties active efforts to improve

D

smoke-removal were going on in the course of the eighteenth century. The same was true of the towns, which had kitchen fireplaces similar to those in the country. It seems very likely that the use of 'hanging chimneys', though not of the inverted funnel type of chimney, spread northwards from South Scotland and to some extent outwards from towns. They are spoken of in Angus in 1746. At Easter Dowald farm on the Abercairney Estate, Stirling-shire, one was valued at 5/- in January 1810. In Banffshire in 1825, an observer noted that they followed the time when there was only a smoke opening in the roof. They reached Shetland by the early 1800s, too. As the movement of the style northwards through the country districts took place, it was at the same time beginning to be frowned upon in the towns, partly because of fire risk in areas of congested housing. Already in 1725, for example, tradesmen in Dundee were being forbidden to build or rebuild any clay, plaster or timber chimneys within the burgh. Although there were such attempts to suppress them in major towns, 'hanging chimneys' survived in smaller towns and villages, as in the North-East until recent times. Such regulations in towns, and the northward spread of the type in the countryside, symbolise the social and economic improvements that had touched the whole country in various ways by the first quarter of the nineteenth century. They were summed up by a writer speaking of hearths in the Highlands in 1824:

> The progress can be traced now in this country, just as it crept on in England; at least when things are left to take their natural course. The fire in the middle of the house is first transferred to the gable; a canopy with a chimney is next placed over it; those who formerly sat near the fire, then sit within the fireplace; in progress of time, this is contracted so as to exclude them; and lastly, this eventful history ends in Carron grates and Bath stoves and registers, in bright brass and brighter steel, the pride of housewives, the dread of chilly guests and the torment of housemaids.

These last-named elements took much longer to reach the crofters' and small farmers' and farm workers' houses, of course. It is also likely that the simplicity of the orderly sequence of the first elements is deceptive. At least, it tends to distract attention from the real variety of hearth-types that existed before and, especially in the kitchen-ends of houses, after the great rebuild that accompanied agricultural improvement. There was the central hearth, adapted in South Scotland by having an inverted funnel fixed above it, and the gable hearth with a wall canopy over it. These two major developments, in their first appearance in South Scotland and in adjacent areas, were made roomy enough for people to sit there in the evening within the space demarcated by the chimneys. Within the open kitchens of earlier times, which served a variety of daily living needs, these canopies marked off especially intimate and cosy areas.

In the same context, another kind of hearth and chimney, of which a small number of examples survives, is of interest. This is what can best be described as the 'hearth outshot', because the hearth has a massive chimney projecting from the gable or side wall of the house, and is itself set in its own living space, with its own small window. It was entered from the main kitchen through a wide, arched entrance. Hearth outshots cover a social spread from medium-sized farms to the homes of small landowners, and date, as far as can be judged, to the seventeenth and eighteenth centuries.

The nearest parallels are the great fireplaces of medieval castles, many of which had projecting hoods in stone, which remained as characteristic features until about the fifteenth century. Within some of these were recesses that acted as buffets or dressers, where displays of plate were laid out. It is evident from this that they were focal points for activities that went beyond simply keeping warm. They provided more intimate spaces within the greater space of large halls or rooms. This is absolutely in line with the purpose of the two main types of canopy chimney, in wood or other light materials, in lesser dwellings. It is as if there was in the minds of the people of the time a concept of a kind of comfort based on the hearth and its surroundings as a place of special importance within the larger and draughtier confines of the kitchen end of old-style, mainly unceiled, houses. This ancient, deep psychological need was expressed in different ways at different social levels by the great stone-hooded fireplaces of castle halls, by the stone hearth outshots at the next social level down, and by the wooden 'Lothian braces' and 'round-about fire sides' of farmers of reasonable means in the better-off southern parts of Scotland. After this kind of social movement had proceeded in time to the beginning of the agricultural revolution, it spread more widely into the country districts where central fires (even if improved by the addition of a back-stone) had been the rule, leading to their eventual disappearance, and to their replacement with 'hanging chimneys', but on too small a scale to serve any purpose other than immediate smoke-extraction. Nor did they have to do more than this, for new buildings were no longer being built with the large, multi-purpose kitchens of the past.

CHAPTER 11

Plough And Spade, Rig and Lazybed

Anyone who wants to understand the older farming system should have some knowledge of the equipment used, which also formed part of the daily and longer-term work rhythms.

Of all a farmer's worldly goods, his plough or means of tilling the soil, and the animal- and manpower required for cultivation, were the most important. In the days before mechanisation there was not, like now, a small number of basic plough types that did their job through the brute force of a tractor, but a whole range of regional varieties, evolved in keeping with soil types and the needs of small communities. Some of them also showed the influence of other countries, like Norway, where tillage needs were similar.

In spite of such variety, the major plough-type was undoubtedly the one often called the 'old Scotch plough'. By the sixteenth century it had developed the working form that continued into the nineteenth century. It was a swing-plough, without wheels to support the front of the beam, long and heavy, with two handles or stilts and a longish, flat, wooden mouldboard. The main iron parts were the sock or share, and the coulter, without which the plough would not work. These were pieces of value, which had to be bought, and which had to be repaired from time to time. There were two chief types of share, one in the shape of a long, pointed wedge, suitable for heavy and stony soil, and for the work of breaking in and reclamation, and the other with a wing or feather at the right-hand side, for under-cutting the roots of weeds and grasses. A pair of socks was part of the kit of the plough.

Though in the eyes of later times this plough-type seemed heavy, awkward and inefficient, the truth is that it had evolved to suit the function for which it was required, which was to plough the soil whether of infield or outfield, into a series of ridges and furrows. The furrows were necessary for surface drainage of the tilled fields; the ridges raised the seed-bed above excessive moisture levels and allowed as good a growth of crops as could be expected in the conditions of the time. It was possible to build up the ridges quite quickly by ploughing up and down on the same strip, always turning alternate plough-slices towards each other so that they

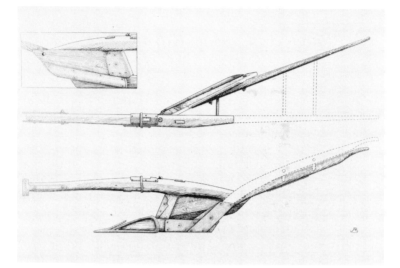

Diagram of an 'Old Scotch' plough. The original came from Chilcarroch, Wigtownshire, and dates to about 1793. It can be seen in the County Museum, Stranraer. It has a four-sided body, and an almost flat, wooden mouldboard. Drawn by John Brown. C1556.

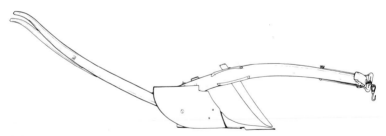

Diagram of an improved plough, with a three-sided body and a curved, iron mouldboard. Drawn by Helen Jackson. C18715.

grew like pairs of cards built one over the other till the required height was reached. Of course, the high ridges of pre-Improvement times were created over many seasons and tended to remain as permanent beds, especially in the infield where mucking was regular. They could be 18 to 36ft. wide and might rise to 3ft. or more in the middle. The width was not a matter of chance. It was related to the spread that could be comfortably sown by hand, and also to harvesting needs.

Diagram of ridge and furrow ploughing, showing the line of the work. The furrows allowed for surface drainage of water. Many examples can still be seen on the lower slopes of hills and where underground drainage is difficult. Drawn by Helen Jackson. C4154.

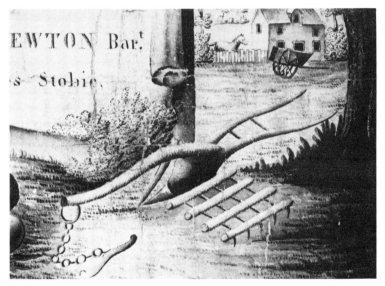

An improved plough, with a harrow and box-cart, drawn on the estate plan of Smailholm Spittal, Roxburgh, by James Stobie, 1777. Scottish Record Office, RHP 3607. C2558. By permission of Tods, Murray and Jamieson, WS.

Since the plough was, in effect, always turning slices of earth up the slope of the ridge, it was always tilted slightly to the right. The long sole acted as an anchor in the base of the furrow, and the long, flat mouldboard pushed up the slice and pressed it into position. The job was not easy, especially in heavy soil or ground that had not been ploughed for some time. That is why the large team of six to ten or even twelve horses and oxen was often necessary, with one man directing the animals and another controlling the plough.

The team was yoked two by two in line ahead. If it was a mixed team, the quicker-moving horses were put in front of the oxen. Horses were always preferred for harrowing. A table tombstone dated to 1753, in Liberton Churchyard, Edinburgh, gives a good impression of the typical work organisation. The plough, working in a field of ridges and furrows, is drawn by four oxen and two horses, with a ploughman and a boy to urge on the beasts. The farmer is sowing seed one-handed from a sheet slung over his shoulder, and a woman servant carries fresh seed to him from a sack. The sown grain is being harrowed in straightaway by double harrows drawn by a pair of horses. The giving of a final ploughing to the seed-bed, with immediate sowing and harrowing so that seed should be well-covered from greedy pigeons and other birds, was a standard routine of the period. The tombstone shows what is evidently a field on an improved, single farm, but the technique is still the old technique, and on a fine sowing day the fields of the old farming communities would have been filled with neighbours, all getting on with the work, and where necessary sharing their animals to make up the full plough-teams. At such times, the fields were carpeted with people at their tasks, exchanging news and scandal and making jokes in the way of working groups the world over.

The heavy plough was used in the major farming districts. There was a lighter version of it, with a pair of very upright stilts, used on higher, better-drained ground, where high-backed ridges were less necessary, along a broad strip of country lying more or less along the Highland Line, stretching from Orkney to Galloway. Its operation was the same as for its heavier brother, but the number and arrangement of the team was different. It was drawn by four — or sometimes six — animals, arranged side by side, and not two by two in line ahead.

This team formation makes a link between the two-stilted old Scotch plough and the one-stilted ploughs of the Highlands and Islands, several of which are still preserved in museums. One was photographed in use on the west side of Lewis in the 1940s. Examples come from Shetland, Orkney, Caithness and the Hebrides. There are several variations in form, because of adaptation to light, peaty soils, and to shallow, stony soils. What is of particular interest for the long survival, in the northern parts of the country, of a plough-type with prehistoric origins, is the way in which trade with Norway helped to keep it going. Merchants taking grain and other goods to Norway in 1652 and 1728, for example, were bringing back numerous plough beams and other wooden plough parts in their cargoes. They would not have done so, however, if the plough-types involved had not been perfectly familiar to the people of Shetland.

Whatever the variety and origins of these single-stilted types, mostly drawn by four oxen or four horses abreast, the fact remains that the work organisation, flowing from the needs of small communities, was no different — except in scale — from that of the two-stilted plough. The ploughmen controlled the plough only, and another drove the team. Different families shared animals to make up a team. Sowing and harrowing were done immediately alongside the final ploughing for a seed-bed. Though the implements differed, the forms of community work organisation had a remarkable degree of uniformity throughout the country as long as the individualisation of farms and farming, which was the hallmark of Lowland agricultural improvements, had not yet set in. The traditional work rhythms, till then, were common to all the rural communities, wherever they were situated.

This world was close to its end by the late seventeenth century, especially in the Lowlands. There were pressures that demanded a much more money-based economy. Cattle, grain and textiles were beginning to produce cash, and the Union of 1707 was making Scots more familiar with English farming methods and equipment. Even before 1750, 'English' ploughs were being tried out by Scottish lairds: people like Barclay of Urie in Kincardineshire, Grant of Monymusk in Aberdeenshire, and the Earl of Galloway who even had a number on his Orkney estate by 1747.

Most of those tried out were the Rotherham make, a swing plough patented in the West Riding of Yorkshire in 1730. Like the old Scotch plough, it was also of wood, except for the sock and coulter, but it was much lighter. By the 1790s, versions of it were in use in most counties of Scotland.

The Rotherham plough was seen and studied by James Small, son of a Berwickshire farmer, who served his apprenticeship as a joiner at Hutton, and worked at Doncaster in the North of England between 1758 and 1763. After this, he settled at Blackadder Mount in his native county and started up a business, making ploughs and other agricultural equipment. He studied the construction of ploughs, and digested his knowledge into a book published in 1784, his *Treatise on Ploughs and Wheeled Carriages*. This technical work symbolises the changing viewpoints of the agricultural revolution.

Small took the old Scotch plough and adapted it by combining with it the main features of the Rotherham plough. By 1767, he was ready to patent his new swing-plough. It had a very rapid spread afterwards, and had a deep influence on Scottish farming. It is one of the 'inventions' that Scots gave to the world, and in fact, by 1803, Scottish ploughwrights were making it at a factory at Engeltofta in Sweden.

Amongst the new features of Small's plough — which set the style of horse-plough that continued till the tractor era — was a curved mouldboard. At first this was made of wood, but about 1780 Small took his wooden pattern to the Carron Iron Company and had it cast in iron. A few years later he also had some other parts of the plough cast in iron. The step to an all-iron plough after that was a short one, and it appears that the firm of Gray of Uddingston, near Hamilton, should get the credit for it.

The strong, but relatively light, form of Small's plough in conjunction with the careful alignment of beam, coulter, sock and land-side to reduce friction through the earth to a minimum, meant that the team could be reduced to two horses. This change was also helped by the fact that by the time the new plough became prominent, and indeed as part of the very steps that led up to its evolution, the old high-backed ridges and furrows were being widely reduced in scale and size. They were levelled and straightened out as the individualisation of farm units proceeded. The landscape of cultivation and the new implement came together, one helping the other. Though Small's plough gets high praise, it was nevertheless only a part of this picture. The 'English' Rotherham plough had become widespread before it, and continued in use after its introduction. There were also rivals like James Wilkie's plough, which, though based on Small, was adapted to the soil conditions of South-West Scotland, especially Ayrshire and Annandale. It was good for stony land, and could plough down rough stubble without choking. Between 1801 and 1812, Wilkie made 2,500 at Uddingston, first in wood and then in iron.

Throughout the nineteenth and twentieth centuries, local

Ploughing with a pair at Lumphanan, Aberdeenshire. AF, 1980.
53.14.7.

smiths and the agricultural engineering firms and foundries that
began to proliferate, continued to produce ploughs modified to
suit local conditions. Smail of Lanton in the Borders, Gray of
Uddingston, Barrowman of Saline in Fife, Brechin Foundry in
Angus, Sellars of Huntly in Aberdeenshire, Banff Foundry and
many others have left their mark on the story of cultivation in
Scotland.

By the middle of the nineteenth century, however, English firms
like Ransome and Howard were beginning to explore the Scottish
market. And from the 1870s, Oliver ploughs from America were
becoming popular. They were cheap, and worn parts could be
quickly replaced. Interestingly enough, the original Oliver was a
man of shepherd stock, from the Newcastleton district of
Roxburgh. Wallace of Glasgow became the main Scottish
distributor. But these ploughs form part of the story of industrial
mass-production. The main point to make here is that with the
two-horse swing-plough, in which the man between the stilts used
reins to control his pair, a new set of farming rhythms was
introduced to the countryside, in such an effective way that
countries around were affected also.

However, not all parts of the country could be tilled with a

Lazy-beds in Lewis, partly dug with spades. AF, 1964. 53.14.11.

plough. This did not mean that no cultivation could be done, and in many parts of the Crofting Counties, the spade and a specialised form of it known by the Gaelic name of *caschrom* were the hand-and-foot-powered substitutes. Digging was by no means confined to these counties. An Act of James I in 1424 tried to establish the principle that every man of simple estate who worked as a labourer should dig, on every work day, an area of seven square feet. There is no doubt also that massive amounts of reclamation work were undertaken by those settled on the edges of improved farms in the early days, with the aid of the spade and with levers for shifting stones. The spade had no mean part to play in agriculture generally, but it is only in the Highlands and Islands that highly specialised forms of spade evolved or remained.

　　Farthest north, in Shetland, special economic circumstances led to an increase in spade cultivation in the course of the eighteenth century. As lairds developed the fishing industry, they reorganised earlier patterns of settlement, so that more men could be housed on smaller units of land. These units were often too small for the plough to operate, or to maintain the number of draught animals required to pull one. The solution was for those left at home, when the menfolk were at the fishing, to make use of the old form of

A crofter at Lochcarron, Ross-shire, using a *caschrom* for planting potatoes. Per Miss A. M. Mackay. C109.

delving spade. It was small, with a straight shaft and a foot peg a little above the rounded metal blade. To use it alone led to little progress, and the practice of team-cultivation with the spade came into being, or perhaps became more common, for it is hardly likely to have been an instant novelty. Members of the team, three or four in number, or sometimes just a husband and wife working together, thrust their spades into the ground at the same moment and levered over a long spit. Years of practice so synchronised their movements that the sight of such work is like watching a well-rehearsed ballet.

In the Highlands and Western Islands, the old spade was more substantial, though its construction was as for the Shetland delving spade. It has the Gaelic name of *cas dhireach*, 'straight' spade. It would be easy to think that it was special to these areas because of its name and associations, but is this true? Two late eighteenth-century writers described it as a 'lugged spade', i.e. with a footstep on it, and one of them said it resembled the 'lugged spade' of South Scotland. There are references to 'foot-spades' in other parts of Scotland also in the sixteenth and seventeenth centuries. There is a good chance that the *cas dhireach*, which also resembles some Irish spade-types, is a survivor of an older spade-form well-known to the folk of the old farming communities.

What is certain is that the *caschrom*, 'crooked' spade, was a native Highland development. It seems to be confined in its distribution to the North and West, and dates back to at least the seventeenth century. It is likely to have evolved in rocky areas, because it is especially suitable for undercutting turfy soil and turning it over, and also for levering up stones. It is a kind of spade and lever in one. In the hands of a skilled worker it is said to have been four times as fast as an ordinary spade. A team of twelve, one working alongside the other in echelon, each taking a step backwards as each spit was turned, could till an acre in a day. A season's work with one, from Christmas till late April or mid-May, could till enough ground to feed a family of seven or eight with potatoes and meal for a year.

Cultivation by spade or *caschrom* goes with a special form of land-use that is well-suited to wet, peaty soils. Instead of the ridges and furrows that characterised the work of the plough, lazybeds were made. They consisted of raised beds with ditches between, made by the spade or *caschrom*. In a way they are a form of ridge and furrow adapted to extreme conditions. On wet land the

The modern ploughman, in the tractor cab. Hamie Barclay, ploughing at Brownhill, Auchterless, Aberdeenshire. AF, 1966. 53.15.3.

technique provided an essential form of drainage that allowed crops of bere and oats to grow with their roots above the water-table.

The making of lazybeds was also a community or at least a family effort. Byre-manure or seaweed was carried in creels on the backs of horses or people, often women, and laid in parallel strips 3 to 4ft. wide, and about the same distance apart. Turf and earth was dug from either side and turned over the manure, and the bed was ready for sowing. In earlier days cereals were grown on them, though after the 1740s potatoes became the main lazybed crop.

It is sometimes said that the word 'lazy' refers to the attitudes of the Highlands. This is not so. It preserves an obsolete sense of the English word, 'untilled', 'uncultivated', and refers to the strip of ground underneath the bed, which was not dug into at all.

Whether the plough or the spade, in whatever of their forms, was the main cultivating implement, the technique of cultivation, using ridges or beds and furrows or ditches, was comparable, as was the need for community work. The nature of the terrain dictated the scale of the approach and the type of tool or implement, and the social system matched also. People and tools and soils were all parts of the same rhythms, differently expressed as circumstances demanded.

CHAPTER 12
Sickle and Scythe

The sowing of seed usually began in April, after the soil had been given its last turn with the plough. The old method was to sow single-handed from a linen sheet, allowing for a one-handed cast that covered half the width of the ridge. In places where crops were sown on lazy beds or in small patches, scattering from a pail or bucket was enough, and there was no need to adapt to the working requirements of the ridge and furrow system. The hopper fixed to the chest permitted two-handed sowing and a double-cast, but by the time it began to be widely adopted in the later nineteenth century, the old, raised ridges themselves had begun to disappear. There had probably been no great need to try to speed up sowing earlier on, for example by the two-handed technique which would have covered a full ridge width at once, since sowing had to be followed straightaway by harrowing or raking by hand to bury the seed out of reach of hungry birds. The operation of sowing, therefore, could not run too far ahead of covering up.

In England, Jethro Tull was experimenting with horse-drawn drills from the early 1700s, and his book on *Horse Hoeing Husbandry*, published in 1733, had much influence for a time. It may have stimulated experiments in Scotland also. By 1760, Mr Craik of Arbigland had produced a seed-drill that sowed grain in rows six inches apart. S. Morton, Agricultural Implement Maker, Leith Walk, was producing a three-drill machine in 1829. Many other makers joined in the efforts to get a really good seed drill, including James Watt of Biggar, Lanarkshire, whose broadcast sowing machine, with jointed seed-chests to allow it to be folded to pass through gates, was shown at the Great Exhibition in London in 1851.

Such seed-drills, some of which put the grain deeper into the ground straightaway, brought the possibility of separating somewhat more widely the operations of sowing and harrowing. On the other hand they also needed a seed-bed that was better broken up than by a final ploughing. As a result, tined instruments like grubbers or heavy harrows, intended to break down clods and make all smooth, came into use prior to sowing, as new standard

Piece-time during wheat-shearing with toothed sickles: detail from an estate plan of Newton, Berwickshire, by J. Stobie, 1777. The shearers have ale, mutton chops and wheaten bread. Scottish Record Office, RHP 353. By permission of Tods, Murray and Jamieson, WS. C4135.

elements in the sets of instruments to be expected on farms.

Outside the bigger farming areas, hand-sowing devices remained in use, supplemented by the mechanical seed-sowing fiddle that came in from America in the second half of the nineteenth century. But even on big farms such items were kept handy for filling in corners and patches where the seed had failed to take or where birds had cleared it out.

There followed a period of waiting, when farmers kept an eye on the green braird, watching it mature into ripeness, and keeping off birds and animals as best they could. By August it was ready for shearing. Quick-ripening varieties were not then available and cutting could go on into late September, or even early October in bad years. By such a late date it was hardly worth harvesting, for birds and mice and wind and rain would have stripped the bulk of the ears.

For centuries the huik or sickle with a toothed cutting edge was the main shearing tool. The teeth were set to saw against the bunch of stalks to be sheared, as the sickle was pulled back towards its user.

In the later 1700s it began to be replaced by a bigger, smooth-bladed type, faster in operation. This change, even in such a humble instrument, is in itself a sign of response to the demands of Improvement. So also was the appearance of local sickle-making workshops, as in the villages of Ochiltree, Banton and Auchin-mully in Ayrshire. England had long been a major source of sickles, with imports through Dumfries and Kirkcudbright in the late 1590s totalling over 4,000, and English makes continued to be imported well through the nineteenth century. By that period, eager attempts were constantly being made to find better or quicker working versions. In the 1830s the Agricultural Museum set up in Stirling by Drummond the Seedsmen had several improved makes on show, American and Russian as well as English. These are clear signs of the anxiety that was felt to find ways of speeding up the shearing, long after the days when agricultural improvements had first begun.

Manpower was a critical factor. Harvesting could be speeded up by better sickles, but increased numbers of shearers were also needed. The change from the toothed sickle, wielded chiefly by women, to the larger smooth-bladed sickle, sometimes called a scythe-hook, used much more by men, was more or less complete by the 1830s in the Lowlands. Men, being in general more powerful, could swing the scythe-hook over as wide a stretch as their strength of arm would allow, getting up to 50% more speed than for the older sickle.

Part of the move to improved harvesting rates therefore also involved a change in emphasis in the work roles of men and women. The seasonal migrant shearers from the Highlands had been predominantly women. After the Napoleonic Wars, male shearers from Ireland started to cross the Irish Channel, called by them the 'Sheugh' or ditch. By the 1820s, there were 6,000-8,000 a year; by the 1840s, with the coming of steamships and cut-throat fares, there were 40,000 a year. The farmers of the Lothians and South-East, of the Forth Valley, south Fife, the Carse of Gowrie, and the Glasgow area, were getting their larger crops cut by better hand tools used by stronger workers.

This was the situation in the big farming districts of the South until after 1850. In North-East Scotland, however, another kind of change was taking place well before then. This was the wide adoption of the scythe for cutting grain crops.

A bandwin team of seven shearers with sickles. One man binds and
stooks to the sets of shearers on two rigs. From H. Stephens, *Book of the
Farm* II (1855), 332.

Scythes were not new to the farming scene, but their purpose
from the time of their earliest appearance in this country in Roman
times was to mow grass and hay. The sickle was the tool for
shearing grain, and not the scythe. Even though scythes figured in
grain-cutting trials in Dumfries, Berwick, the Lothians, Fife,
Angus and elsewhere in the 1700s and early 1800s, the experiments
were short-lived and farmers stuck to the sickle.

In the counties of Moray, Nairn, Aberdeen and Banff, farms were
smaller than those farther south, and extra manpower was both
less easy to get and harder to pay for, because farmers were less
well-off. There was a great increase here in the arable acreage also,
and the need to speed up the harvest was just as essential. The
solution was to use the scythe for grain to an extent that had never
been known before in any country. From about 1805 onwards, the
North-East, with its characteristic form of scythe with a Y-shaped
sned or handle, led the world in this innovation. It may not seem
much to us now, but it meant a great deal then. By the 1850s, the use
of the sickle had almost vanished from the North-East, except
perhaps for the shearing of wheat, the ears of which were thought
to be too easily shaken by the scythe. Wheat was the most valuable
commercial grain, and no one wanted to risk reducing the yield.

For the first half of the century, therefore, the North-East was
more advanced than the South, because the farmers of the South
had to depend on the annual floods of seasonal migrant labourers
whose implement was the sickle, not the scythe. These long-

distance travellers could scarcely have been expected to carry scythes on their shoulders. The older, traditional grain-shearing tool, the sickle, remained the major means of cutting the southern hairsts, as part of a system that farmers could not break out of until the coming of mechanical reapers.

Modifications in hand tools led to changes in techniques. From the mid-1600s, shearers are known to have worked in teams called bandwins. Increasing grain acreages must have sparked off the formation of such teams. They were mainly of seasonal workers, who had to be paid in cash and not in kind. The farming economy had to reach a stage where it could bear the cost of their employment. The bandwin system of team harvesting is a true mark of the beginnings of agricultural improvement in the leading grain-cropping areas in the seventeenth century, and of a growing emphasis on cash as a medium of payment for work done.

Too much should not be made of such points. They only hint at change, which was limited in its extent by the available tools and techniques and by the social system. The organisation of the bandwin team had to suit the techniques of cultivation. It fitted the plough ridges. Characteristically, two ridges were worked at a time. Three, or sometimes four, shearers, male and female, moved along each with their sickles. The one on the crown of the ridge, usually a man, had the additional job of making straw bands, which he threw on the ground. Another man following bound and stooked the sheaves for both ridges. The ridges averaged 15 to 18ft. wide and each shearer cleared a width of 5 to 6ft. A rate of 2 to 2½ acres a day was possible for a bandwin of seven people.

As a rule several teams worked together, and on big farms seventy or a hundred people could be seen bent over their sickles at the height of the season. Human nature being what it is, it is not surprising that George Hope of Fenton Barns in East Lothian should have written in 1834: 'managing thirty-four and thirty-six rigs of shearers is, I assure you, a pretty tiresome job'.

In smaller farming areas there was another, much looser, form of organisation for harvesting. The system allowed for more individual work. Each according to ability worked along the ridge. The farmer employed a bandster to tie the sheaves and set up the stooks for his shearers, in threaves of twenty-four sheaves of oats or barley, or twenty-eight of wheat. Payment was according to the amount cut.

Scything corn at Ness in Lewis, 1979. The scythes have Y-shaped sneds.
Per Ness Historical Survey. C7775.

This threaving or gang system was especially common near
towns and villages that acted as reservoirs for day-labourers and
others who were anxious to make what money they could at this
busiest of all farming seasons.

On small farms, and where extra seasonal labour was hard to get,
the work had to be done with the existing labour force, helped by
the wives and families of farmworkers and local tradesmen,
domestic servants, and anyone else who could be got. As long as the
old farming communities existed, it was this kind of collaborative
effort by all hands that got the crops in.

The cutting technique with the toothed sickle was to work along
the line of the ridge. The coming of the smooth-bladed sickle led to
a system of working across sets of ridges. This could only happen
after groups of ridges had begun to be blocked together in
individual fields. It is a mark of the bite of Improvement.

The scythe also operated across the ridges, with the scythesmen
working in echelon. It was hard to use a scythe if the ground was
stony and lumpy, and its adoption must have greatly speeded up
stone-clearance as well as the levelling and smoothing of plough-
ridges. It brought also a modified form of work-organisation.
Scythers had to be strong men, capable of standing the fatigue of
long days. Strapmakers made the straw bands, and female lifters

A 90 year old, Mr
Aitchison, Ettrick Muir,
Selkirk, with a straight-
handled scythe. AF, 1966.
53.16.15.

gathered the cut swathes into sheaves and laid them on the bands. A
male bandster followed, tying and stooking the sheaves. In the
South, where the climate sometimes allowed sheaves to be bigger,
women gatherers often used a lifting pin in the form of a metal
hook or small wooden rake, to extend the reach of their arms. A
man or woman with a large rake worked behind the groups, taking
up loose heads of corn. Three scythesmen and their followers were
expected to move quickly enough to leave work for one raker.

Since the limitations on rapid harvesting due to the use of hand
tools were critical, the rates of production are worth looking at. A
shearer with a sickle was expected to reap a quarter to a third of an
acre a day, working a twelve-hour day. On a big farm, calculations
for the number of people to hire were based on a rate of eight to ten
acres a head over a period of sixteen to twenty days. If the farm was
near a town, shearing was done by the piece, at 4/6 to 5/- an acre in
Berwickshire, but much more expensively at 7/- to 8/- an acre in
Angus. This greater cost marks the greater scarcity of seasonal
labour north of the Tay, and helps to explain the pressures that led
to the adoption of the scythe in the North-East, as a means of

avoiding the payment of high wages. It is also true that the shearing period tended to be longer in the North, as a result of poorer weather.

A scythesman could cut two acres of oats, nearly two acres of barley, or a little over two acres of wheat, in a ten-hour day. Not only working time and manpower were saved, but also drying time, for scythe-cut sheaves were more open. More straw was got, too, for the scythe cut lower than the sickle.

Savings in time, wages and in the cost of food supplied show clearly why the North-East adopted the scythe for grain. The real paradox is that the sickle was kept for so long in the more advanced farming areas, largely as a result of the very scale of operations that enforced dependence on supplies of seasonal migrant labour. They were forced to comply with the traditional skills and the traditional tool, the sickle, of that labour force, even though they did what they could by using male Irish rather than female Highland labour, and smooth-bladed rather than toothed sickles, to expedite the work. By the mid-nineteenth century there were no improvements left to make in the existing situation. Mechanised reaping must have seemed like a dream of heaven.

CHAPTER 13

Reaper to Combine

In 1803, the Highland and Agricultural Society of Scotland, reflecting the concerns of its members, offered a prize for the invention of a reaping machine. Two years later, Mr Gladstone, millwright in Castle Douglas, Kirkcudbrightshire, produced a machine with a rotary cutter equipped with a number of toothed sickles. The same principle was followed by Smith of Deanston, Stirlingshire, in 1812, when he tried but failed to win a £500 prize offered by the Dalkeith Farming Club. The concept of sickles was difficult to get away from, and in any case, horses could not push the reaper fast enough for rotary cutters to operate efficiently as on modern tractor equipment.

Credit for what is certainly one of the great agricultural achievements of the nineteenth century must go to the Angus divinity student, Patrick Bell, son of an Auchterhouse farmer and later minister in Carmyllie. He evolved the principle of mechanised scissors as a basis for a new type of cutting blade, of the kind that remains to the present day on reapers, binders and combine harvesters. This blade was a major advance, first fitted to a model in 1827, and to a full-sized machine in 1828. By 1832, at least ten of

A reaper with a rotary cutter, by Smith of Deanston, 1812. From J. C. Loudon, *Encyclopedia of Agriculture*, 1831, 422. C4038.

114

A version of Bell's reaper made by Crosskill of Beverley. From a poster dated 1853. C3936.

his machines were at work in East-Central Scotland, and examples had been exported to America, Australia and Poland.

The breakthrough had been achieved in principle, but there was a big stumbling block to its widespread adoption at home. Bell's reaper was long and heavy. It was pushed into the crop by a pair of horses, and worked well when the line was straight, but it was awkward to turn. The biggest problem was that even though farms and fields had been individualised, it was still necessary to use the ridge and furrow cultivating technique, since systematic, underground tile drainage had not yet begun to provide an alternative to surface drainage. The reaper, therefore, had to jump awkwardly across the corrugations of the ridges, or work along them on a slope. It was before its time. The ridges of the farming landscape had to be levelled out before it could be freely and widely adopted. Another technical problem was the lack of back-up services. Smiths and joiners were not yet equipped or trained to keep reapers in repair, nor was there any reservoir of spare parts.

Meantime in America, a young Virginian farmer, Cyrus McCormick, was developing the reaper that came to bear his name. Patented in 1834, it was the first machine that could be called fully practical in all respects including manoeuvrability. The McCormick works, set up in Chicago in 1847, developed into The International Harvester Company, which was turning out 10,000 reapers a year by 1871.

Back in Britain, McCormick's machine, as well as the much

simpler American Hussey, and Bell's reaper, were shown at the Great International Exhibition in London in 1851. They aroused tremendous interest, and made people in general aware of Scotland's pioneering role. The English firm of Crosskill of Beverley started to make a version of Bell's reaper and for a time this was popular. In the end, however, the lighter American reapers won the day.

What was the reason for the delay in adopting the Scottish reaping machine in the main grain-producing areas of Scotland, when farmers were so hungry for some such invention? The ridge and furrow contouring played a role, as well as servicing difficulties, and the very high cost of investment in drainage to level the ground. These were enough to delay widespread adoption.

Tile drainage and ridge levelling were going hand in hand from the late 1820s. Tile works were springing up by the 1840s. An Act was passed in 1840 to allow landowners to raise loans for drainage, Peel's Public Money Drainage Act of 1846 offered loans to be repaid over a 22-year period, and the Private Money Drainage Act of 1849 led to the setting up of several private companies to finance drainage and land improvement. The result was a farming and landscape revolution, in the middle years of the nineteenth century, that created the face of farming Scotland as we know it, and set the course of Scottish agriculture, with well-drained level fields on which new and improved horse-drawn equipment, rollers, harrows, seed-drills and, above all, reaping machinery could be worked with ease.

Drainage on this scale, with its accompanying effects, was as much of an achievement as Bell's invention of the reaper, and it had to come before the reaper could be readily taken on. By the time the work of draining and levelling was far enough advanced, the light, manoeuvrable American makes were in full production. They were the ones that made headway on farms throughout the country, rather than the native Scottish breed.

The mechanical reaper did not solve all problems at once. It still used up a lot of labour. The cheapest reaper, the Hussey, cut into the crop and left a swathe that had to be gathered and made into sheaves to clear the path for the next run. To keep it cutting at the rate of an acre an hour, something like sixteen workers were needed in the field. It was too costly in both price and manpower for

Harvesting with a binder in Roxburgh. 6.50.9.

smaller farmers, and for this reason scything remained the main means of cutting in North-East Scotland till the 1870s and later.

The Bell and McCormick reapers could, however, lay the swathe clear of the next run. Gradually, technical improvements were made, like mechanical or side delivery of cut grain, which began to reduce labour requirements for the reaper.

The next important step was the coming of the string-tying binder. McCormick in the States, and Walter A. Wood in Birmingham, had produced examples by the late 1870s, and T. B. Bisset and Co. of Blairgowrie, established in 1862, had their own self-tying binder by 1890. By this date, the binder-twine knotters could be adjusted so that the size of sheaves was regulated to suit the condition of the crop. Manpower needs were again reduced, for there was then no need to gather the grain and bind it into sheaves by hand.

Finally, the combine harvester reached Scotland in 1932. It was designed to cut, thresh and dress grain at the same time, and completed on the field the threshing operations that had formerly been a regular weekly burden on the farm workers for a great part of the beginning and end of every year. It therefore not only saved time in handling the harvest, but also left more time free for other jobs later. The first machine was a Clayton, introduced by Lord Balfour at Whittingehame Mains in East Lothian, where one of the country's earliest corn-driers was also installed to cope with the great flood of grain that flowed in from the fields in a wonderfully short space of time. This combine harvester is now in the collections of the National Museums of Scotland.

The combine harvester was one of the major pieces of equipment that marked the coming of a new world. To be cost-effective, it needs big, open fields, not subdivided by fences, dykes or hedges, and fully mechanised back-up equipment. All of this makes for heavy investment, for a machine that works during only a few weeks of each year. As a result, its early adoption was slow, and limited to bigger places. Smaller farms came to have access to combine harvesters through contractors. Its spread goes on in the Crofting Counties: a Massey Ferguson reached the farm of Bigging in Rendall parish, Orkney, in 1950, and the island of Papa Westray got its first one in 1973.

CHAPTER 14
Harvest Home

The relentless speed of the combine harvester has been removing, slowly and almost unnoticed, the stooks from the fields and the stacks from the stackyards. The harvest countryside no longer looks as it did even a generation ago. The wide variety of shapes and sizes of stacks that once marked the different farming regions has gone for ever.

Even the sheaves and their tying bands once had much variety. Climate affected size: a Lothian sheaf could be 12in. across, an Angus one 10in., in Banffshire they could be 10in. or 7½in., and in the moist Hebrides 5 or 6in. These differences affected the techniques of tying the band also, for in the Lowlands the job was done on the ground, but in the Highlands it was done against the worker's thigh.

In the old farming community, the way of tying the band was important, since it served as an ownership mark. There are sixteenth and seventeenth-century cases of stealing sheaves 'of other men's bind', from Shetland down to Ayrshire, and as recently as the 1920s sheaves in North Ronaldsay, Orkney, could be

Fields of stooks at Dunblane in the 1690s. From Slezer, *Theatrum Scotiae*, 1693. LIB/1571.

119

identified after a gale because of the individual bands of two farms. This is the kind of small detail that characterised the community farming days of the past. Binder-twine began to replace straw bands in the late 1870s.

An old way of setting up sheaves of oats, also known in Ireland and Northern England, and suitable for wet conditions, was to stand them singly with the tail well spread out and the band tied high up near the head. This was a gait. It could be made of a single thick sheaf, or of two or four together, bound separately and also with an extra band round their tops. This method was probably very widespread until the eighteenth century. It lasted longer than that, but by then the familiar arrangement of six to fourteen sheaves leaned against each other in line, with or without hood-sheaves on top to run the rain, had become normal. Possibly this kind of stook originated or spread with the coming of the bandwin teams in the seventeenth century.

In areas of small crofts and rough terrain, and in pre-Improvement days, the crops were often carried on the human back to the houses, in bundles of sheaves roped together, or on the backs of ponies. In the high-farming districts, mainly south of the Tay, two-wheeled long-carts for transporting grain or hay were on the go from the first half of the seventeenth century. Farther north, where farms were smaller, the box-cart became the standard harvest-cart, adapted for the purpose by the addition of an overlapping wooden frame. It is not a matter of chance that the old-style gaits were convenient for back-transport, whilst stooks suited bigger-scale operations including forking up to a builder on a harvest-cart. The harvest-cart and stooks alike mark changing days and a new tempo.

In wet weather, and if the butts of the sheaves were very grassy, small temporary stacks might be built in the field. In Skye the name *gurracag* was used, in Orkney the screw or dess, in South-West and Central Scotland rickle, and in the South-East, the dash. They could be taken home at leisure to be built into full-sized stacks, or else threshed straightaway.

As grain production increased in the eighteenth century, much attention was paid to stacks, and to means of keeping them dry and free from vermin. It became common to build stacks on raised stone foundations, a practice first noted in Angus in 1768. From the early 1800s, engineering firms were taking advantage of the demand by

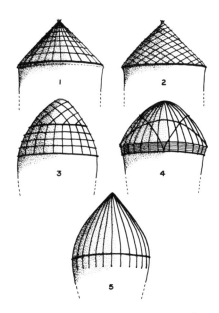

The shapes of stacks and roping methods: 1–2. From Stephens, *Book of the Farm*, III (1844, 1096, 1094; 3. Half net-work, half-lozenge roping. From a sketch by A. Anderson, Aberdeenshire; 4. A Border method. From Stephens III (1844), 1096; 5. An Orkney style. From a sketch by W. S. Moar. C3972.

producing cast-iron foundations. In areas of smaller-scale farming such costly items were rare and foundations were often little more than a pile of old straw, brushwood or broom, spread on the ground if stacks were being built at the side of a field near the buildings, or on the circular stone cobbling of the stack-sites in the permanent stackyard at the back of the barn.

In the Northern and Western Isles, stacks averaged about 7ft. high by 5ft. in diameter. They were built as cones that started to narrow, after the first few ground courses, to a pointed top. There is little doubt that these tell us what pre-Improvement stacks looked like more generally in Scotland, but already by the late seventeenth century a degree of sophistication in stack-building was evident in the richer areas. Illustrations of 1693 for Linlithgow, Dunfermline, St Andrews and Ross show neat stacks with round, upright shanks topped by conical hats; at Stirling, however, there was a type with a relatively narrow foundation, and a shank that swelled out to the eaves. This variety, and the implication of pleasure in building stacks well, is a further pointer to the seventeenth-century beginnings of agricultural improvement.

Just as sheaves varied greatly in size from north to south, so also did stacks. In South-East Scotland, by the 1850s, stacks of oats and

Round 'screws' of oats, and rectangular 'desses' of hay, at Biggins,
Papa Stour, Shetland. AF, 1967. 53.16.13.

barley were about 15ft. in diameter, and of wheat, up to 18ft., over
three times greater than in the crofting areas. They might even, in
more recent times, be built as rectangular sows, which is
unthinkable farther north. They were so big that an extra forker
was needed, standing on a ladder, to get the sheaves up to the man
building the stack. Between North and South, stacks were mostly
similar in shape to the small stacks of the North and West, but
bigger in scale.

Once the stacks were in they were prepared for winter days by a
cover of thatch, well roped down. In latter days nets came in handy
for keeping the thatch in place, and just before that ropes of
coir-yarn or of twisted binder twine were used. The older way,
however, was to make straw ropes for this purpose.

The twisting of ropes was one of the crafts practised by all farm
folk. It was never a specialist job. All it needed was a device to twist
the straw, a simple tool that had numerous different forms and
names throughout the country. One man turned the twister, most
commonly called a thrawcrook, and another undertook the more
skilled task of 'letting-out', i.e. feeding the stalks evenly through
his fingers into the rope as it formed. This was a fine job for days
that were too wet for work in the fields. The completed ropes were
coiled into round or oval balls that were stored on the couples of
the grain loft or barn till the time came to use them.

Though not a specialist craft, rope-twisting was nevertheless

Stacks in Fife, one crowned with a cross. C3909.

acknowledged as a skill to be proud of. At agricultural shows, there could be rope-twisting competitions. In particular, the making of the oval shuttle-shaped balls of straw rope required much ingenuity. The reason for this shape was that one of the ways of roping thatch involved taking horizontal ropes round previously placed verticals, to finish up with a pattern of squarish meshes. The oval balls were made to take the horizontals under and round the tightly-held verticals. With round balls, on the other hand, the placing of ropes was from shoulder to shoulder, and the result was a diamond-shaped mesh. The roping and general finish of stacks became a matter of great prestige and pride, an art form in itself, even though — like a beautifully presented dish at table — it was made only to be destroyed.

The finishing touch given to thatched stacks was to make a tuft on the crown, the peerie, or else to make a straw cross. These decorative features were common in Central Scotland.

When all the grain crops had been led in and the stackyard was full, the men might get a dram, but the main moment of celebration was the end of shearing. Much of the total effort of the farming year went into preparing the soil for bearing crops. To reach the stage when a ripe crop was completely cut and safe from

E

storm, birds and vermin was a moment of supreme satisfaction, well worth celebrating, and well worth offering up thanks for in church.

The last stalks to be cut were bound into a sheaf or given a human shape, or tied into the form of a cross, and hung in the kitchen or laid on the byre rafters. In mechanised days the last sheaf bindered might be kept too, though the custom no longer continued as a natural extension of a long tradition. The use of the last sheaf varied. In Argyll, it was often given to the horses when they began to harrow or plough. In the North-East, the clyack-shafe, or maiden as it was called south of Aberdeen, was given to the best milker in the byre, the first calved cow, or a mare in foal. Latterly it was shared out amongst the beasts at Christmas or the New Year. In parts of Orkney this was still being done in the 1920s, probably under the influence of North-East farmers who moved there in the second half of the nineteenth century.

It is a curious mark of the Lowland-Highland divide that whereas farming districts treated the last sheaf with honour, in the North and West it was treated with disdain. The last handful cut might be thrown into the field of a neighbour who had not yet finished, as a kind of insult, and it then had the Gaelic names of *cailleach*, 'old woman', or *gobhar bhacach*, 'lame goat'. In parts of Orkney not influenced by the North-East, efforts were made to avoid being the one to cut the last stalks. Men struggled also to avoid being the last to get the grain into the yard, and competition was furious down to the last load. For the one who failed, there was the disgrace of a figure in the shape of a dog, the bikko, 'bitch', put on the cornyard gate to greet him. Those in the yard barked in derision as he arrived. Traces of a similar desire to avoid being last also exist in Shetland.

The Lowland approach demonstrates satisfaction at a job well done. It was rounded off with a social gathering called the kirn in the South, the meal an' ale in the North-East, and the muckle supper in Orkney. Why was the approach so different in the crofting areas in general? Grain-producing farmers were celebrating as all men wish to celebrate to mark a good occasion. The crofters, however, because their ways of life remained closer to the old community farming system, continued to have other sets of values. In a joint-farming group, certain basic tasks had to be or should be begun and finished at the same time by all. The move to

A large stack at the farm of C. Riddell, Peaston, Ormiston, East
Lothian, on an iron foundation. AF, 1963. 53.16.9.

the shielings, the sowing of crops, the harvesting and transport of
crops off the field, are examples. The last was especially necessary
because the stock returning from the hill should have full range
over all the unfenced fields of the farming village, gleaning what
they could. One who was slow in clearing his crop was delaying a
major activity common to the whole community, as well as the
follow-up grazing that, in effect, turned all the arable into part of
the common grazing. Derision at a slow worker, as marked by the
cailleach, the *gobhar-bhacach* and the *bikko*, is not so much a
piece of curious folklore about whose pagan origins people may
speculate, as a piece of functional psychology aimed at maintaining
conformity and keeping a system going. The straw figures and
shapes of the farming districts may derive from those of earlier
days, but have been completely transformed to match individualised farming. The attitudes to the last grain cut in the Crofting
Counties point straight back to the ways of the older communities.

CHAPTER 15
Threshing

For centuries the rhythmic thumping of the flail marked the darker months of the year. Just as the speed of hand reaping was a bottleneck before mechanisation, so also was the rate of threshing. Hand threshing involved long hours and it took time to release grain from the stalk for use as animal feed, as nourishment for people, and as a trade item. Although there were some options other than flail threshing, none were speedier: grain, especially oats whose ears shake readily, could be threshed by striking the sheaf, held upside down, with a notched stick; the rubbing out of ears of barley with the bare feet was a known Hebridean method; more widespread than these was the custom of lashing sheaves against a suitable object, like a stone built to protrude from the barn wall, a block of wood or rung of a ladder studded with nails, or an open frame with iron cross-bars. Such small-scale means of threshing survived because they had a special purpose, that of keeping the grain stalks as long and unbroken as possible so that they could be used for thatching buildings more efficiently. The flail would have broken up the straw too much.

The flail is a two-piece instrument, consisting of a handstaff and a beater or souple linked at one end by tough, pliable thongs of eel-, sheep- or goatskin or the like. Ash or larch was good for the handstaff, and ash, hazel, thorn or any wood that did not split easily for the beater. The latter could also be of tarred rope or animal hide, especially for threshing oats, which bruised more easily than bere.

Throughout the country there was great variety in the names for the parts of the flail, including the joining band, in the proportionate lengths of the two main pieces, and in the ways by which the joining band was fixed. Setting aside detail, however, Scottish flails divide into two broad groups, a Lowland type with a leather cap on the beater, and a Highlands and Islands group with either a hole or groove on the head of each of the parts. One particularly interesting example with a pin through each end to act as an anchor to the joining band has survived till recent times in Orkney. This form was used in South Scotland in the 1840s, and

A flail with pins to retain the joining-band, held by Mr. Gaudie at Netherskaill, Orkney. AF, 1968. 53.15.61.

there is no doubt that it travelled up from there and across the Pentland Firth, though leaving no trace of its passage in between. It is one of the many indicators of the good standard of Orkney farming, which was moving well beyond the 'crofting' bracket from the mid-nineteenth century onwards.

The essential buildings in the old community were the house, byre and barn. The barn was where flail threshing went on, sheltered from the elements. For this purpose, the couples had to be high enough not to get in the way of the souple as the flailman swung it up, ready for a powerful down stroke. There was also a special threshing floor, the simplest form of which was the clay spread over the threshing area of the barn. A good clay floor made for a cleanly operation. Most barns had two doors opposite each other, between which winnowing was carried out to clean the grain, and the clay floor was laid just to one side of the space between them. Sometimes square wooden threshing platforms were used, with their joists resting on top of the earthen floor, or sunk into it. On such floors, one or several folk worked with the

flail, till enough straw had been prepared for animal feed or until
the limits of storage space for grain and straw had been reached.

The steady beating noise penetrated the early morning dreams of
young folk still in bed, whilst their elders sweated in the light of a
flickering lamp in the eerie shadow-filled barn. It is no surprise
that stories of supernatural threshing with the flail abounded.
Such lore and imaginings are also parts of the old rhythms.

Just as a greatly increased grain acreage drove cutting with the
sickle to the limits of its possibilities, so also did it affect threshing
with the flail. The search for a speedier means of threshing was no
less eager than that for reaping machinery. For reaping, early
experiments involved rotating sickle blades; for threshing, it was
rotating flails.

Mechanisation of threshing by attaching flails to a turning beam
was tried out by one Michael Menzies about 1732, and by Mr Craw
of Netherbyres, Berwickshire, around 1750. More promising was
the line explored by Mr Stirling of Dunblane, Perthshire, and
others in the 1750s-60s. They adopted the principle of a water-
driven flax-mill, with four scutchers turning in an enclosed
cylinder into the top of which sheaves were fed. Riddles and
fanners then separated grain and straw. Although the system
worked for oats, it was less good for other grain crops. All the same,
several such mills existed in Kinross-shire in 1814, and they were
said to have been fairly common across the Border in Northumberland by about 1800. They worked much faster than the flail, and
might well have spread even more widely if something better had
not come along.

Experimenting continued in the 1770s and 1780s, until Andrew
Meikle of Know Mill in East Lothian succeeded in producing the
world's first fully successful thresher in 1786. Meikle was a member
of a remarkable family, the activities of which reflect the
excitement of this phase of the Improvement period, when
agriculture and water-powered industry were still going hand in
hand. His father, James, built the first barley mill at Saltoun and
was responsible for the first winnowing machine, Andrew's son
George later erected the huge water-wheel that drained Blair-
drummond Moss, reclaiming much now fertile land as a result.
Andrew died at the age of 92, at Houston Mill in East Lothian,
having given to the world of agriculture one of its most essential
pieces of machinery. The principle was simple: the spread-out

A farm with a horse-walk, middle left, where the horses walked in a circle to drive the threshing mill. C13148.

sheaves were fed through a pair of fluted rollers into a revolving drum that knocked out the grain. The straw was then carried clear by drums with wooden teeth, which were probably fitted soon after the initial invention.

The first mill was set up for Mr Stein, distiller at Kilbagie, Clackmannan. It included fanners to separate the chaff from the corn. Such was its success that orders for more mills followed quickly, and Meikle set up about a dozen in the same district.

The need for such a machine hardly needs to be stressed. Farmers provided their own testimony, for mills mushroomed throughout the length and breadth of the country. By the 1790s they were numerous in the main cropping areas. At the same time the new trade of millwright burgeoned. John Nicol of Stonehaven made eight mills in six months in 1795. John Gladstone of Castle Douglas built 200 between 1794 and 1810, at from £40 to £130 each. Farther north, the diffusion went more slowly, though Sutherland had ten by 1811 and examples were to be found on the larger farms in the islands of the Hebrides.

Just as the reaping machine spread internationally, so also did the mill. A Manx farmer set one up in the 1790s. They were common also on Swedish farms by 1800. The estate of Dowspuda in Poland had two Scottish mills by 1817. Scottish agriculture was making its mark in Europe.

In the new farming revolution that is upon us, the threshing mill has itself become redundant, having been displaced by the combine harvester. Its traces are less easy to sweep aside. They still leave a widespread mark on the farm architecture of the country, in a range of forms conditioned by the motive power. This was of three kinds: wind, water and horse.

There was a scatter of threshing windmills in the country, for example at the farms of Bankhead near Forfar, Dumbarrow near Dunnichen, and Bolsham near Kinnell, all in Angus, and at Montbletton, Gamrie, Banffshire. Some small ones were tried in Orkney. In general, though, wind was too uncertain a servant, and the more controllable power of water and of horses was preferred. The outcome was the addition, after the 1780s, of new features to farm steadings. Water power required lades and mill-dams with sluice gates, and water-wheels alongside the barn walls. Horse power led to the building of circular horse-gangs beside the barn. On smaller places, for example in North-East Scotland, they consisted simply of raised platforms, round which one or a pair of horses walked, turning by means of a shaft the gearing in the middle, which then conveyed power through an underground beam to the mill inside the barn. On bigger places generally, but especially in South and East-Central Scotland, hundreds of attractive tile- or slate-roofed horse-gangs appeared. The roofs stood on pillars, between which were open spaces to let air through freely to the sweating horses, up to six in number according to the size of the mill. In fact, more horse power was needed for earlier mills, which were big and stiff to drive. Only after millwrights had learned to refine them and make them smaller did they begin to spread to medium-sized farms. Many of these enclosed horse-gangs remain on farms throughout the country, as also in the North of England, adding a strong element of visual interest to the farm buildings, even though, for the most part, the side-openings have been filled in, the gearing has gone, and they do service as storage spaces.

As horse- or water-powered mills spread down the social scale of farms, the bigger grain-producers went on to take advantage of industrial techniques. Steam power began to be used in the 1830s.

Threshing with the traction engine in South Scotland. Per Mrs A. Scott. C4285.

By 1845, there were two steam-driven threshing mills at Ratho in Midlothian, and one at Inveresk. Their effect was to introduce great steam boilers erected on plinths and tall brick- or stone-built stacks to the architecture of farms.

New technology led to further change by the early 1900s. Steam, a cumbersome medium because of the size and cost of installation, maintenance, and fuelling with coal, was replaced by the oil-engine. Firms like Allan of Aberdeen made engines with heavy fly-wheels in their thousands. To house them, engine sheds were built alongside the barns. These too began to be phased out, as tractor power came into use during but mainly after the First World War. The tractor pulley could do all that was needed to drive the mill, by means of a simple shaft and pulley protruding through the barn-wall. Since 1786, threshing technology has thus created a series of building changes, from mill-dam and horse-gang, to smoke-stack and engine-shed, and then to wall-pulley. Finally, the combine harvester has done away with the need for barn-mills altogether.

This, however, is not the full story. There was also an infrastructure to serve the needs of places unable to cope with the costs of expensive items. This involved help from contractors, and the making of smaller-scale, hand- and foot-operated threshing equipment by local firms. In fact, there was often a half-and-half kind of situation in Scotland. Though local contractors came around with travelling mills drawn first by horses from farm to farm, then by traction-engines and then by tractors, farmers nevertheless liked to have their own threshing machinery whenever possible. Even if the barn-mill or hand-thresher was used for the weekly winter thresh, to keep up a supply of fresh straw and bedding for the byre and stable, the travelling mill would still be ordered for a bigger-scale thresh each year. This was in itself a kind of community event, where farmers neighboured with farmers, and the farmers' wives fed the assembled company of workers. The use of portable mills goes back to at least 1864, when James Smith of Dalkeith was advertising one.

Hand- and pedal-operated threshers began to be made soon after 1830. They came to replace the need for threshing with the flail on small farms and crofts. Firms like Shearer of Turriff in Aberdeenshire, and Banff Foundry, made large numbers for local use, for the Highlands and Islands, and for export to other countries such as Portugal about the period of the First World War. Even this modest threshing device made its mark on the wider world.

CHAPTER 16
Kilns and Mills

Scotland, with the sea around, has a moist climate. Ears of grain have to be artificially dried before they can be ground, otherwise they would not granulate into meal. Drying was especially needed for oats. Bere or barley could be ground without drying in a good season because the ears were naturally hard, but if malted to make ale, it had to be dried to stop the growth of the shoots.

Not every farm or even every community had a specially-built kiln, and a number of small-scale ways of drying grain evolved over the centuries. An old method called graddaning, a name that goes back to the 1500s, was known in the eighteenth century in Galloway, the Highlands and Western Islands, and North and North-East Scotland. It involved setting ears of oats on fire and burning off the stalks and chaff. No threshing was needed. In 1578, Bishop Leslie described how the Highlanders ground the oatmeal in hand-mills after graddaning, and then made it into a kind of thick oatcake. This was baked on a girdle above the fire, or laid against a baking-stone set at the side of glowing peats.

Graddaning was a picturesque job that was left to the women. Two worked together beside an open-air fire of chaff. One set fire to the ears of a handful of corn, watched until the chaff had been burned off, lit another bunch, then dashed the first against the ground to extinguish it. The other spread the ears with a stick to check that they had been burned clean and were well parched, then raked them into a heap. When enough had been done, the heap was put into a tub and the women trod it with their feet and rubbed it with their hands to remove the charred particles. Winnowing followed, and the ears were then ready for grinding. In places like Skye, Uist and St Kilda, this technique still survived in the nineteenth century as a means of making fresh oatcakes from the first grain cut during the new harvest season. It must have been a treat eagerly looked forward to. However, it was not only a Highland phenomenon, for a form of graddaning was used in Moray at the same period, though at an inside fire.

This was one technique evolved by the old communities, and there were others that varied according to the type of grain. Oats

Grinding with a handmill in the Highlands, early 20th century. A handful of grain is being put into the eye of the quern. I. F. Grant Collection. C7172.

could be graddaned, or, if threshed out, the ears could be parched in a pot, in a container with a flat stone base and clay sides, or in a straw basket. In the last case, hot stones were dropped into it. Bere, however, could be dried in the unthreshed ear in an openwork net over a peat fire, or laid on a big iron girdle, as happened in Old Aberdeen in 1699. Bread-girdles were also much used for this job in Norway.

Such methods, though testaments to human ingenuity, were for small-scale purposes. They were not always markers of poverty, for their use was widespread, and by no means confined to Scotland. Graddaning, for example, was forbidden by law in seventeenth-century Ireland, on the grounds that it was wasteful of straw. If carefully done, however, the bulk of the straw could be saved, and cattle would not have objected greatly to its burned ends. There is no doubt, though, that the straw was often completely burned.

Built corn-drying kilns were everywhere very numerous. Most of the old communities had one or more, and many can still be seen in deserted settlement sites. In parts of Shetland a small, rectangular type was built into a corner of the barn, but elsewhere kilns were usually circular, with a round drying floor and an egg- or bowl-shaped drying chamber. The heat from a peat fire was carried along a straight or curved flue, and allowed to rise through the drying floor. This consisted of spaced, wooden slats over which a floor of straw was laid as a bed for the grains. In many parts of the Crofting Counties, in the Glens of Angus, and in other higher-lying areas of settlement, kilns were often built into slopes or banks, facing the direction of the prevailing wind. They remain as stout, stone-built structures, easily identifiable by the round bowl in the centre. In other cases the kilns were built into small kiln barns, within which winnowing could be done in shelter. On bigger farms, notably in Orkney and Caithness, they were more substantial, and also built onto the end of the barn. The survival of many into the present century may well be due to a fondness for home-brewed ale, for which the malt had to be dried in the kiln.

In Lowland Scotland, kilns were also common, in towns as well as in the countryside, but they went out of use with the spread of new commercial meal-mills, to which relatively big corn-drying kilns were attached. From the 1780s, kiln floors of metal and of perforated tiles were coming into use, which greatly reduced the fire risk from the old floors of wood and straw. The new kilns also used chaff in their fires instead of peat, and so they brought to an end the heavy flavour of peat that must have characterised most of the meal eaten up to that period.

Once the grain had been dried, it was ground with equipment whose scale matched economic and environmental circumstances. In museums and in private gardens, knocking stones abound. They are like large mortars in which bere or barley was dehusked with a stone pounder or a wooden mallet, to prepare it for making barley broth, a widespread element in the everyday diet. The knocking of bere was regarded as a woman's job, and it could happen that the stone was shared by several members of the community.

A horizontal mill in Papa Stour, Shetland. The water wheel turns in the opening below. About 1890. Per Lady Linda. C12964.

The interior of a horizontal mill at Collafirth, Shetland, showing the hopper and grindstones. About 1890. Per Lady Linda. C12968.

For centuries, bere was prepared in this way. Then, in 1710, Andrew Fletcher of Saltoun in East Lothian sent James Meikle (father of Andrew, of threshing mill fame) to Holland to study barley mills. On his return he erected a barley mill at Saltoun, making pot barley, the fame of which spread far and wide, but the secret of how it was dehusked to produce a pearly appearance was long kept a Fletcher secret. Two more barley mills were built in East Lothian in 1753-4, and a few years later, around 20,000 bolls of pot barley were being exported each year. Barley mills spread in the Lothians and Fife, and for a time Scotland had quite a lucrative monopoly of the trade, until barley mills began to be built in England, Ireland and America. This, however, was a very different level of activity from the humble knocking stone.

The rotary quern or hand mill was available for grinding grain from probably just before the time the Romans came to Scotland. Though examples can still be found on crofts, they had, in general, reached the end of their span by the middle of the nineteenth century. Estates in some areas tried to make sure that all grain was ground in the official mills, so that dues would have to be paid, and from time to time efforts were made to prohibit the use of hand mills or to break them up. Even the central authority of the Scottish Parliament laid it down in 1284 that hand mills were not to be used except through stress of weather or where water mills were lacking, and for the next 500 years both estates and town councils kept repeating such prohibitions, but clearly without permanent success. There were some estates that did not apply such regulations, especially where water was scarce. It could also happen, for example in Harris, that the better-off used water mills, and the 'lower orders' used hand mills. Hand querns were even preferred for certain purposes, such as making barley meal, even if their owners were sending their oats to the water mill.

Water-operated mills are amongst the most fascinating pieces of machinery known to man. The hiss and splash of water on the rapidly turning wheel, the rumbling of the stones and rattling of other working parts make an unforgettable impression, as does the taste and aroma of meal freshly off the stone and still warm. Technically also, they have a satisfying quality.

The simplest form is known as a 'horizontal' mill, because the water-wheel turned in a horizontal plane immediately below the grinding stones. In practice they are adaptations of the hand mill

Mill of Newmill,
Auchterless, Aberdeenshire.
The sluice gate is open; the
water does not turn the
wheel until it is closed. AF,
1962. 53.15.49.

to water power, for the wheel turned the top stone by means of a ·
shaft without any kind of intermediate gearing. Probably evolved
in the Mediterranean area in the 1st century BC, they had reached
Ireland and perhaps Scotland about sixteen hundred years ago,
before the Vikings came.

Their known distribution in Scotland is in the North and West,
from Shetland down to Galloway, and then on to the Isle of Man
and Ireland. It is likely that they were at one time more
widespread, but the evidence is not clear. As they stand, their siting
is strongly affected by climate and geography. They were found on
hilly or sloping terrain, being very numerous in some areas by the
early 1800s. When Sir Walter Scott visited Shetland in 1814, he
spoke of 500 such mills there, and even allowing for poetic licence,
there must have been many. One example has been preserved at
Dounby in Orkney by the Historic Buildings and Monuments
Directorate of the Scottish Development Department.

The horizontal mills were, for the most part, built by members of
the small communities they served. They did not usually form part
of the organisation of estates that ensured that dues from grain

The Mill of Newmill interior. AF, 1962. 53.15.51.

ground flowed into the purses of the lairds. That function was left to the much bigger-scale vertical mill.

Vertical mills were to be found wherever grain was grown in reasonable plenty, including the North and West, and in particular Orkney, but their main distribution was in the Lowlands. They were very much part of the feudal organisation of estates. In towns as well as in the country there were common mills serving districts, in which the tenants were bound by the terms of their lease to have their grain ground. Under this system of thirlage tenants paid a proportion of the meal ground, the multure, to the proprietor or to the tenant of the mill. They also had to help in the upkeep of the mill, the mill-dam and the lade, and in the getting and transporting of new millstones when they were needed. It was a tight piece of organisation, in itself a reminder that estates were as a rule well-organised units, easily capable of taking on board and implementing the changes necessary to bring about the agricultural revolution, once enabling legislation had been passed in the late seventeenth century.

All the same, a dour opposition to constraints is part of the nature of country folk everywhere. The estate mill was seen, subconsciously or otherwise, as an enforced point of contact with a

The miller's wife: Mrs
Aggie Anderson, Mill of
Newmill, Auchterless,
Aberdeenshire. AF, 1960.
53.15.11.

system that required them to part with a proportion of the grain
they had worked so hard to produce. It is not surprising that hand
mills kept on working, however surreptitiously, for over half a
millennium after an Act tried to stop them. Nor is it surprising that
the miller, as the man who represented the estate, should often have
been unpopular. There was a strong suspicion that millers never
came off worst, and that the mill swine were better fed than those of
other tenants. In the words of the proverb, 'the miller's soo's aye
best fed'. Millers and the estates tried so hard to ensure that dues
were paid, that in Stitchill in the 1660s it was decreed that wheaten
bread for penny weddings should be ground in the estate mill and
not bought ready-baked in the town markets. At the same time, the
malt for the bridal ale was also be be ground in the estate or barony
mill.

The mill, one of the focal points of interaction between estates
and tenants, is one of the clearest means of demonstrating how the
old communities, though self-organised to a great extent as a result
of centuries of adaptation to particular environments, were also
subjected to superimposed forms of authoritarian framework,
which could involve a good deal of communal activity in the
upkeep of the mill.

It is not likely that all such work was resented all the time. The
cleaning out of a mill lade gave fine opportunities for getting eels
or trout for a tasty meal. There was probably a lot of pleasure, too,
in extracting millstones, a real mixture of craftsmanship in
carving them out of quarries, and hard work in transporting them,

on edge, with a wooden beam through the middle. Many local millstone quarries existed. The coarse sandstone rocks of Pennan were much used in the North-East. There were quarries, for example, at Cowie in Kincardineshire, near Glamis in Angus, at Kaim Hill, Fairlie, Ayrshire, and many more. Already by the 1490s, there were four 'miller-quarriers' at Dunbar, which was one of the centres from which grain was exported by sea.

Native millstones began to go out of use in the early nineteenth century, however, as the import of French burr blocks was started by firms such as J. Smith & Co. of Edinburgh, established in 1823. The practice developed of building up millstones of keyed segments. Such composites were more economical, and they quickly helped to bring to an end the old community-based need for quarrying entire stones.

CHAPTER 17

Neeps an' Tatties

Both turnips and potatoes were first grown in the late seventeenth century as novelties in the gardens of proprietors, often spreading from garden to garden as related families and friends passed on samples to be tried out. Family relationships played a great role in the early diffusion of these and other plants, as well as types of trees, in the days before the easy, instant and general transmission of new knowledge through the media. Lord Belhaven's comment that chives and leeks were not for common folk suggests also that they valued and were careful of such knowledge of rarities.

In the course of the eighteenth century, the new root crops moved from the gardens to the fields, and became fully integrated into the economics of Improvement. They provided food and fodder for man and beast, they became an element of wages paid in kind, they led to general upgrading in the quality and size of animals by allowing them to be overwintered in good conditions, they stimulated the trade in fat cattle, they helped to clean the land they grew on, they permitted new kinds of rotations that could keep the land in good heart, and they sparked off the development of a new range of horse-drawn equipment for making and cleaning drills. Turnip sheds were added as integral elements to new farm steadings. The farming landscape was itself embellished by fair fields full of straight, neat drills, bare in preparation for the roots they were to foster, or clothed with the green shaws of the growing plants. The widths of drills were adapted to the width of cart axles, so that movement up and down, as when lifting pulled turnips, could be smoothly done. Root crops brought a major new rhythm into the farming year, and left their mark on the face of the land and on the form of farm buildings.

Turnips were being stolen from the garden of the Laird of Urie, Kincardineshire, by 1672, and the Laird of Mayen, in his sheltered lands by the Deveron, was ordering seed from Patrick Lawson, merchant in Banff, in 1693. By this time they had already become part of the trading circuit.

By the 1740s they were a field crop, at first sown broadcast, in East Lothian, Berwick and Roxburgh. The Marquis of Tweeddale had an English land steward who used them to feed wedders. Drills were at first made about 6ft. apart to allow horses to work easily between them, though they soon settled down at 22 to 30in. apart. This allowed a single horse to walk between them, and seed barrows could sow two drills at a time.

To begin with, drills were made with a single mouldboard plough, which cut a furrow slice first one way, then the other, so that the two furrows leaned against each other. This doubled the work, and it was not long before drill-ploughs with symmetrical, double mouldboards appeared. Once the drills were made, muck was carted to the field and spread in the drill bottoms. The next stage was to split the original drills, making new ones where the manure lay under the crop to be grown.

The preparation of land for turnips was labour-intensive. It was ploughed about November, cross-ploughed in March or April and harrowed to break clods and clear weeds, twice ploughed between May and June, and again harrowed and cleaned. After this, the drills were made. Sowing took place in early June of the two types that became common, the softer yellows and the hardy, reddish Swedes that liked a touch of frost.

Various sowing devices were used. One called a bobbin' John, said to have been invented by Mr Udny of Udny in Aberdeenshire around 1730, consisted of a metal cylinder with openings on the end of a wooden handle. It was rolled along one drill at a time. Seed-barrows with a pair of handles and a single hopper, pushed by one man, remained common on small farms for some time, especially in the north, though horse-drawn sowing machines dealing with two drills at a time were being used on the bigger farms from the 1780s. The difference in cost was considerable, indicating the difference in status of the users: in 1812, a one-drill hand-barrow cost £1.6/- and a horse-drawn two-drill seeder, £8.8/- or more.

The need for drills led to the appearance not only of drill-ploughs to make them and of seeders that sowed on them, but also of equipment to clean them. Although the ordinary light plough and the drill plough could themselves be used for scraping the drills and cleaning off weeds, nevertheless there quickly sprang into being a range of drill harrows and horse hoes, supplied by agricultural engineering firms and by local blacksmiths. Old cartwheel rings were often recycled for such purposes.

Women hoeing turnips in Fair Isle, Shetland. The men were at the fishing, and the plants had grown rather big before being singled. AF, 1962. 53.15.45.

The cleaning of drills with horse-drawn equipment made it easier to hoe the turnips when the young plants had grown big enough. Hoes were sold commercially or could be made of a length of scythe blade mounted at right angles on a long wooden handle. The spacing or singling of the plants allowed for a final cleaning of the whole drill, so that the day's work ended with a stretch of drills perfectly free of weeds, with neatly spaced plants. It was a source of great pride amongst farm folk that their drills should be well-rounded and smooth, even though shoulders ached after a long day of standing at nearly the same angle.

In autumn and through the winter, when the stock were housed, the plucking and storing of turnips went on as a regular task, whatever the weather. An iron hook was used to pull the turnips from the ground, and a blade sliced off the tops and tails. If drills were hard-frozen or deep in snow, a stouter, double-pronged pluck was needed to hoist them out. Drills were pulled two by two and the turnips laid so that a horse and cart could move between the twin rows. These could readily be thrown into the cart, the sides of which were raised by means of wooden shelvings to increase the body capacity. A well-trained horse would move forward and stop

Planting tatties. The drills are opened, muck is spread along them, the potatoes are planted, and the drills are closed. From H. Stephens, *Book of the Farm*, II (1844), 660. C1634.

as required at the command of one of the men filling turnips from each side of the cart.

Turnip husbandry marked what became the main cattle-feeding areas, like the North-East, and Orkney after the 1820s. In the Borders another technique was more common. This was sheep country, and crops of turnips were used to feed the flocks for five or six months in winter. They were eaten off the field. This practice continues, but turnip work was so intensive that cattle farmers have been glad to discontinue it in favour of easier options like silage.

Potatoes were being grown as a field crop near Kilsyth as early as 1728, but this was exceptional. Till about 1750, they were mainly to be found in gardens. It was in the Highlands and Islands, however, that they made the greatest impact on the everyday life and economy. South Uist and Benbecula had them by 1743 and then they spread, slowly at first, in the course of the following quarter of a century. By the 1770s they were to be found everywhere. It appears that the original cost of introduction was borne by lairds like Clanranald and by gentlemen tenants.

From this period, they became the basis of subsistence in much of the Crofting Counties. The small fields and lazybeds where oats and bere had been grown were increasingly turned over to the growing of potatoes, and there was an accompanying spread in the making of lazybeds for this purpose. Potatoes were said to have taken the place of bread for up to two-thirds of the year, which must surely point to a decline in the amount of land under grain crops.

The spread of the potato and the great extension of lazy-bedding coincided with the wide displacement of the inhabitants from their old settlement areas, as sheep took over. From the point of view of the lairds, the moving of the farming villagers to the coasts was a practical arrangement that left the hills and straths free for the development of sheep farms, and it brought the men close to the sea, where a fishing industry was being developed, as well as the burning of seaweed in kilns to make kelp. As the men were more and more tied up in such tasks, the women had to take on many of their farming functions. Though men usually dug the lazybeds, it was the women who carried byre and seaweed manure in creels on their backs, who planted the potatoes, and later saw to their lifting with the mattock-like *croman* or the hook-shaped *crocan*. These hand tools seem to have appeared with the adoption of the potato as the major food crop.

As long as the potato flourished and the yield was plentiful, people could survive. Fishing and kelp work gave cash returns that helped to pay rents and buy meal, but if the potato failed, the basis of subsistence disappeared, and the cash income was not enough for alternative means of survival. By the 1830s, potatoes constituted 75-88% of the diet of Highland families, as against a Lowland figure of 25%.

A recession in the kelp industry, an increasing centralisation of fishing on a limited number of ports, and years of potato blight in 1835, and worst of all in 1845 and 1846, all worked to create a desperate situation, to remedy which Government action had to be taken. A Famine Relief Committee was set up, and continuing Government intervention became more and more necessary. This was the period when hungry families migrated in their thousands to countries across the sea and to the towns and cities of Britain, there to be absorbed in completely new ways of living. It is as if dependence on the potato had become too great, though if there had been no potato famine it is doubtful if matters could have carried on indefinitely without outside help.

In the Lowlands, the potato also played a very important role in the diet of poorer folk, though not to such an overwhelming extent. As a rule it formed one element in the diet only. During the nineteenth century it came to be given as part of a married servant's wages, either as a direct allowance or as permission to plant a certain quantity. It found its own niche in the general system, without taking over the system itself.

In the farming areas potatoes were planted in drills as for turnips, though fewer preliminary ploughings were necessary. They were also planted in lazybeds in an interesting way. The tenants who took up holdings on the moorland edges after the individualisation of farms were encouraged to make lazybeds for potatoes on rough land, old pasture and wet soils. In this way, from the 1770s, the potato played a part in the reclamation of land.

Farmers, in advance of the Town Council allotment system, were already letting patches of ground to tradesmen and others around villages and towns by the 1780s. This was especially common around Alloa, Clackmannan, Dollar, Tillicoultry and Menstrie. The need for food in cities was already leading to responses by the 1790s, when Mr Graham of Kilsyth, for example,

Spinner tattie-diggers outside the smithy at Blackhill, Eassie, Perthshire, in 1910. Per J. Johnson. C10537.

was growing potatoes for the Glasgow market. The urban demand stimulated the increase in the acreage of potatoes grown.

At first they were not integrated with the rotational system. Their function in reclaiming land was recognised, as also was their usefulness in providing cheap food for farmworkers. Even in East Lothian, by 1794, potatoes constituted a third of the food of the 'common people'.

In addition, they had a wide use in feeding horses, cows, poultry and pigs, and in some areas, including Fife but with the main emphasis on South-East Scotland, they laid the basis for a great expansion in pig-rearing. Other districts followed suit, like the Nigg area of Ross-shire, though when pig prices fell in the mid-1840s, the potato acreage dropped sharply.

On lazybeds and in the cultivated patches of small-scale farming areas, planting was often by means of dibbles. In the Lowlands and on big farms, potatoes were planted by hand in drills. Mechanical planters to replace such patient hand work began to appear only in the 1930s, though even after that their rate of adoption was slow.

Lifting was done in parts of the Highlands by means of the *croman* or *crocan*, but already by 1800 the three-pronged graip or fork with slightly flattened prongs was in use everywhere. Graips were also common in the main farming districts, though it was more usual to split open the drills with a drill-plough to ease the work of the 'tattie-pickers' or '-howkers'. Some of the drill ploughs were fitted with sets of fingers that lifted and spread the tubers, making them cleaner and easier to gather. In 1855, the spinner digger was patented and later improved by Wallace & Sons of Glasgow, and several other firms were producing their own makes by the end of the century. Experimenting continued, for this was heavy work for which seasonal labour had to be hired and housed annually in the main potato-producing areas, and farmers were hunting for equipment that would reduce manpower needs. In the 1920s the elevator digger appeared as a further step, and more recently potato harvesters with large gridded wheels that clean as well as lift. Nevertheless the difficulty of mechanically separating potatoes, stones and hard lumps of earth — and there have even been attempts to do so electronically — made it impossible to avoid using the hands and eyes of men and women. At the harvesting seasons in the Lothians and Angus and elsewhere, numbers of 'tattie-pickers' are still required in season, although the wartime

Riddling tatties at West Pilton, Midlothian. Per J. Watt. C2599.

custom of giving school children a 'tattie holiday' to help to get the crop in has now been given up.

The storage of potatoes brought further new features to the farm. Potato pits appeared, well covered with straw and earth to give protection from rain and especially frost, which could make potatoes rot into a black, slimy mass. In the little island of Papa Stour in Shetland there were picturesque, half-underground 'tattie-hooses', about 12ft. long by 7ft. wide, with stone side walls and a roof of timber and thatch like a normal house. Similar ones, but bigger, about 15ft. by 8ft., were built in Fife around 1800. There were even stone-built underground pits, like prehistoric earth houses, built with much skill. Examples were known in Roxburgh and Fife about 1794-1800, and some can still be seen, though long out of use, on farms in the valley of Glenesk in Angus.

Since the potato reached Scotland, countless varieties have come and gone. Disease has always been a problem, and major efforts have gone into developing disease-free strains. Orkney had specialised in this already by the 1850s. The common Orkney red was exported as clean seed to Shetland, Leith, London and the Isle of Man. In Angus, prominent potato men like William Paterson of Dundee imported potatoes from several countries and developed disease-free varieties like the Victoria, marketed in 1863, and the Champion, marketed in 1876. Archibald Finlay of Markinch in

Fife produced the Up-to-Date in 1891, and thereafter the British Queen, the Majestic and the Eldorado. From 1918 the Scottish Board of Agriculture started the field inspection of crops to try to stamp out disease and maintain the country's reputation in the world as a good source of disease-free potatoes. Seed potatoes became and remained a prominent part of the Scottish contribution to farming.

With the adoption of turnips and potatoes as important elements in the farming economy, and the appearance of the associated equipment and buildings, the pattern of development of Scottish farming in the nineteenth century reached a point at which it remained as long as horses provided the main power, until major technological changes began to make their presence felt between the Wars.

CHAPTER 18

Milk, Butter and Cheese

Cattle, sheep and goats produced a range of valuable products. These were meat, hides and skins, wool and tallow, and milk. Milk is a perishable commodity. When processed into butter and cheese, its life was much extended, and its commercial value greatly increased.

Until the end of the eighteenth century, milk regularly came from sheep and goats as well as cows. In the manuscript Court of Session Extracted Processes, there is a reference, dated to between 1532 and 1538, to the profit from 63 ewes, amounting in butter and cheese to a value of £6. In 1666 Sir John Skene of Hallyards, Midlothian, was making comparisons. In his view, cows' milk was best for butter, and ewes' milk for cheese. Cows' milk gave more and better butter than ewes' milk, and ewes' milk more and better cheese than cows' milk. Each type of milk, however, was clearly in common use for both purposes, though ewes' milk butter was of secondary quality. It had a wide use as grease, and for mixing with tar to smear sheep before the system of dipping them in disinfectants started.

Milking a cow in Uist. Cathcart Collection. C1737.

A milkmaid in 1777. From an estate plan of Newton, Berwickshire, by
J. Stobie. Scottish Record Office, RHP 3553. By permission of Tods,
Murray and Jamieson, WS. C4134.

By about 1800, the milking of ewes had more or less come to an
end. It lasted longest in the Lammermuirs and the head of
Annandale, where farmers continued for a time to milk ewes to get
butter for sheep-salve, and cheese to sell to shops. In the
Highlands, Samuel Johnson observed the milking of both sheep
and goats in 1775. If the goats' milk was not used in liquid form, it
was made into cheese, either by itself, or mixed with ewes' milk and
sometimes warmed cows' milk. The milking of ewes took fifty
years longer to die out in the Highlands than in the Lowlands, and
then mainly because of the Clearances. Even so, it was not
uncommon for Blackface sheep to be gathered into fanks or pens
once or twice after the lambs had been weaned, to get their milk and
keep the households supplied with cheese. In Rannoch and the
Braes of Lochaber, goats went on being kept for milk and cheese.

But cows were and remained the main source of milk, and it is
their milk that is referred to in the bulk of the historical sources.
The degree of official interest is underlined by the appearance of
butter and cheese in early charters and rentals, and in grants and
regulations of the Acts of the Parliaments of Scotland from the

Mrs Williamina Robertson feeding a calf in Fife, about 1890. Per Miss M. Blyth. C3073.

time of David I in 1147 onwards. James VI forbade the export of cheese in 1573. Charles II, in 1661, required 2 oz. of bullion to be brought to the mint for each 5 cwt. of cheese exported. Under William in 1701 and Anne in 1705, the import or use of Irish, English or foreign butter was forbidden.

Butter and cheese figured so regularly in the payment of rents that the word 'kain', which means a payment in kind as part of the total rent, came to have the meaning of a quantity of cheese amounting to about 60 cwts. This was in Argyll, Ayrshire, Dunbartonshire and Galloway. In these areas, the dairyman who paid his rent in cheese was called the 'kainer'. The church teinds or tithes also included butter and cheese. It was from rents and teinds that the bulk of what was used for trade came, and the extent of the trade is clear from the degree of central interest in it.

The demands for these valuable food items by church and estate can scarcely have failed to reduce the dietary standards of country folk in the centuries before the introduction of the potato, though the problem may have been less in the Highlands, where milk products were considered to be plentiful. It was said in the early 1600s that the Highlanders, who lived solely on milk, cheese and flesh, were able to supply cheese to the Lowlands at times when cereals were scarce there.

Milk products were much more of a mainstay before the growing of cereals began to dominate the Lowland farming economy. In the twelfth century, the Acts of the Parliaments of Scotland laid down a toll of a halfpenny for a load of butter or cheese on horseback. Carriage in panniers on horseback, therefore, was a regular means of moving such goods. Within Scotland, there was a good deal of movement of supplies to centres of demand. About 1800, quantities of butter shaped into globules were carried in open boats from Caithness to Moray, where it enriched the pastry of the bakers' shops in Elgin and Forres. Normally, however, it was carried and stored in containers. At the same time, Moray was also buying butter and cheese from Banffshire. Cheese was being brought into Scotland for the larders of lairds like Grant of Monymusk, who by the 1730s was getting quantities of Cheshire and Gloucestershire cheese from Farquharson and Lesley, the Aberdeen merchants. When a traveller dined at Brahan Castle near Dingwall in the 1780s, he noted on the breakfast table fine-flavoured butter, fresh and salted, and also Cheshire and Highland cheeses, 'the last very indifferent'. It seems as if a touch of disdain had appeared in the lairdly attitude to local cheese. At any rate, the more costly imported English cheese would not have been for lesser tables.

That trading in cheese was well organised is shown by the existence of a cheese warehouse near Gray's Close in Edinburgh in 1790. Whether or not it was a staging post for cheese from England is not known. Small traders were active in selling cheese, as well as

Ayrshire cows at Colm's Day Fair, Largs, on 17 June 1913. Per Mrs S. D. Mensing. C2890.

butter and eggs, in the market stands long before then, in the early 1500s, and 'cheeseman' was a recognised designation.

The scale of demand was high. On the Monymusk estate in the 1700s about 3 lbs. of cheese a day was used, or 1095 lbs. a year. Butter was absorbed at an even higher rate during the summer months when it was fresh and plentiful. Towns and cities encouraged production in the areas around. Berwickshire farmers as well as hinds were selling firkins of salted butter in Edinburgh, Berwick and Dunbar by the 1790s, and cheese and kits of salted butter were being sent by Renfrewshire producers into Glasgow. Ayrshire had already been developing its reputation by the 1660s, though Sir John Skene of Hallyards did not think that the cows' milk cheeses made in Cunningham were good. He still preferred his ewes' milk cheese. However, Ayrshire cheese grew in fame and its influence spread. By 1812 Mr Traill of Hobbister in distant Caithness was making Dunlop cheeses for sale in Edinburgh, using Ayrshire cows and employing Ayrshire dairywomen.

Butter also had its recognised dealers, the 'buttermen', a number of whom are named in sixteenth-century Edinburgh sources. In fact, the tron for weighing butter in the capital, from the 1400s onwards, was called the Butter Tron, and the 'butter market' was a well-recognised institution. When not used fresh, there was an assortment of containers for longer-term storage and transport —

F

Mrs Helen Stout, Busta, Fair Isle, using a plunge-churn. AF, 1962.
1.29.23.

firkins and kits, bowies, barrels and kists, and earthenware mugs.
The storage space needed for these commodities alone, in cheese
lofts and butter rooms and in less specialised areas, including army
provision stores, was very great, and had to be able to cope with
seasonal influxes at the times when rents were being paid. Butter
and cheese mountains are nothing new.

Just as countrywomen in Central Europe at the present day go to
town markets to sell small quantities of vegetables, fruit, flowers
and other items from their gardens, so also the countrywomen of
Scotland took butter to local markets. They sold it fresh, and to

keep it cool they would wrap it in a rhubarb leaf, or immerse it for a time in a well. A number of 'Butter Wells' were so named as a result. The butter of earlier times should not be judged by the standards of the present. If it was paid in rent, people were not particularly careful with it. But poor-quality butter found its market also, for sheep farmers used it with tar as a salve in smearing sheep till around the 1850s. From Peebles to the Northern Isles, the process of 'hairing' butter was known — i.e. of taking a knife blade through it several times to remove hairs.

The old way of churning butter was to put it in a small wooden tub or earthenware pot covered with a tightly tied sheep- or goat's skin. Tipping this forward and back, sometimes for several hours, eventually induced the milk to break. Shaking in a leather bag was also done, and a Moray method, said to have lasted till about 1770, was to whisk the milk with the bare arm in an iron pot.

These were ways that the women in the old farming communities had to invent if they did not have the more costly upright plunge-churns. Such 'kirns' needed bigger amounts of milk at one time. They were common everywhere from the 1400s onwards. They were items of enough value to be noted in the lists of goods left by deceased persons, whether in town or in country. They were in the form of tall, stave-sided tubs, with or without a lid, in which milk was churned by the up and down motion of the plunger-like kirn-staff. By the 1790s, patent barrel- and box-churns that rotated on a stand had begun to replace plunge-churns, though in smaller-scale farming areas these remained until well within living memory.

Cheese was made using a variety of materials as rennet, like the stomach of a calf, lamb, hare, deer or sow, or the gizzard of a fowl, or plants like autumn crowfoot. The solidified curd was broken up, often with the fingers, and lightly salted, though evidently salt was not always easy to get. The little ewes' milk cheeses of St. Kilda, and the goats' milk cheeses of Jura, were sometimes cured with the ashes of seaweed, and barley-straw ash was also used on occasion. It seems to have been normal to make cheeses without salt in the Highlands, and to salt them afterwards for a few days in a wooden keg.

Soft cheeses and crowdie were eaten soon after making. They were hung in a cloth to drip and to dry a little in the air. For cheese to be kept longer, pressing was essential to get rid of all the whey.

(Left) A granite cheese-press at Mill of Aucheen, Glenesk, Angus. Drawn by John Brown. C4043. (Right) An iron-framed cheese-press at Delnamer, Glenisla, Angus. Drawn by John Brown. C4045.

A moveable screw-press, with a *chessell* in position. At Braeminzion, Glen Clova. Drawn by John Brown. C4044.

For this a wooden cheese-vat was needed. The cheese was wrapped in a cloth, and as pressure was applied to the lid, the whey was squeezed out through holes in the sides. Pressure could be through laying on stones of gradually increasing weight at regular intervals. Most of the older presses were of long planks, wedged at one end, and with weights laid on at the other. There were some large ones in the main cheese-producing areas of Renfrew, Ayr and Lanark, capable of being operated by the 1790s. In Roxburgh, ewes' milk cheeses could be made up to three stones each in weight, and some of the store farmers were making 200-300 stones each year. Screw-operated stone cheese-presses first appeared in the South-West and spread after about 1800 to other parts of the country, remaining in use for the next two hundred years. Cast-iron presses on the screw or steelyard principle were also common in South-West and East-Central Scotland.

Stone and iron cheese-presses went with the days when most of the milk was processed on the farms. At the time of the First World War, large creameries working on pooled milk supplies were set up, and the need for home-processing on a large scale gradually came to an end. Grocers' travelling vans, themselves now almost things of the past, also began to carry commercially produced cheese and cheese imported from abroad to all parts of the country. Considering the past importance of home-made cheese, it is likely that at no time for five or six hundred years has less cheese been made in Scotland than at present, in spite of efforts to boost Scottish cheeses in the delicatessen and superstore markets.

The only Scottish dairy breed of cow is the Ayrshire. It evolved in the eighteenth century on the small dairy farms of the South-West. Its ability to produce milk from fodder that was only moderately good meant that it was ideal for answering the demand from the rapidly growing industrial towns. In turn, wherever there were such urban centres, farmers in the vicinity set about acquiring Ayrshire cows. As a result, Ayrshire or Dunlop became what might be described as the national cheese. It was a mild, sweet-milk cheese, which kept its place till the 1850s, when the Cheddar system of cheese-making was introduced from Somerset.

The South-West was responsible for another development. Cheshire cheese had been coming from England since the early 1700s, and, no doubt under this stimulation, an Annandale laird encouraged Cheshire people to settle on his estate in Dumfriesshire to make Cheshire cheese there.

With such a strong emphasis on milk in the South-West, it is not surprising that the area played a part in the development of milking machinery. Experiments had been taking place in Germany, Denmark, Sweden and America from the 1840s.

In 1891 Stewart Nicholson of Bombie in Kirkcudbrightshire invented teat-cups made of cows' horns, with india rubber cushions. These were connected by flexible pipes to an airtight milking pail from which air could be drawn by a pump. Suction

Cheeses drying at Orphir, Orkney. They were made with a metal Don cheese-press. AF, 1962. 53.15.27.

was continuous, however, as it was for another machine made by William Murchland of Kilmarnock in 1889. The pulsator principle that allowed the teat-cup to imitate the natural sucking action of a calf was finally evolved about 1895 by Dr Alexander Shields of Glasgow. His Thistle Mechanical Milking Machine was the basis for J. & R. Wallace of Castle Douglas's Kennedy and Lawrence Universal Cow Milker of 1900. This was the first fully practical milking machine. In this way, the milk-producing South-West made its mark on the world of farming, just as the arable South-East did at an earlier date with Small's plough and Meikle's thresher, and the arable East with Bell's reaping machine. All the major elements of the farming economy were being actively and successively pursued.

Butter and cheese played a very wide role, both locally and nationally, but milk in itself, being perishable, was at least as important in the everyday diet. What was not converted into butter and cheese was consumed locally. Since the right to keep a cow applied to most members of the pre-enclosure communities, it cannot be doubted that milk products, fresh or preserved in some way, were the main form of defence against hunger, as long, that is, as the cow was in milk. Probably one reason for cossetting the cows in 'longhouses' where byre and dwelling area were next to each other was precisely in order to encourage them to stay in milk as long as possible, for the sake of their owners and their progeny alike. Even under the new farming regime, the farm servants, in cottar house, bothy or chaumer, all had a milk allowance, and in this way an emphasis on the use of milk in the rural diet was maintained.

Necessity can make people very ingenious. Even fresh milk, or failing that, whey, could be processed to make it go farther. It was first boiled in a pot over the fire, then a stick with a cross-head, round which horse-hair was bound, was twirled rapidly in it, between the palms. This raised a strong froth, hence the name 'fro' stick'. According to an account of the 1690s, frothing up was done five or six times, and the froth was supped off the top with spoons each time. Sometimes this was a food when little else could be got in hungry times, and sometimes it was made as a pleasant drink. The sour, thick milk underneath cream could also be frothed up into a cooling drink. On the East Coast from Moray down to Angus, a mixture of cream and whey was worked up with the fro' stick and sprinkled with oatmeal. There was a rhyme telling how to do it:

> Not too high, not too low,
> Not too fast, not too slow.

Since the use of a frothing device covers much of Scotland, and not only the Highland areas, it is likely that it was fairly general in early times, and the dish of frothed milk with it.

When a cow had newly calved, the first, and sometimes second, milking was put into a dish, flavoured with salt or sugar, and warmed till it set to a custard-like consistency. In later days cinnamon was sprinkled on top. The custom of making 'calfie's cheese' in this way may not be very old, however.

Much more traditional was a practice commonly carried out in Shetland and Orkney. Hot water was added to buttermilk just out of the churn, producing a white, cheese-like substance. This was hung in a cloth. The liquid left over was drunk fresh, or could be kept. It was called bland. When kept for a time in barrels, it fermented to a sparkling stage, when it made a refreshing drink and was recommended as a cure for consumptives. It was the drink taken to sea by Northern Isles fishermen when they were on the water for some time in their open boats.

In the same islands there were various preparations of coagulated or soured milk, for drinking or eating. Sweet milk was deliberately curdled by adding sour milk or buttermilk. New milk might be boiled for hours till it became thick, brown and clotted. It took a lot of milk to produce only a moderately-sized dish.

It is a matter of interest that in Shetland, where plenty of other milk products are or were to be found, there is almost no tradition of cheese-making after the eighteenth century. There, milk rather than cheese was a normal part of the rents paid, and although those who received the rents no doubt processed the milk into butter and bland, cheese was certainly not one of the outlets. In general, the practices of the Northern Isles are in line with those of Norway.

The general pattern for milk and milk products is double. At the level of community consumption, a great deal of ingenuity is shown in making them go a long way at times of necessity, and in evolving ways of utilising — and preserving for shorter or longer periods — residues like whey which in the better-off dairying and farming areas were fed to pigs or poultry. Some of the practices must be very old, and they emphasise the importance of milk and its products in the daily diet. At the level of trade based on milk products assembled through the payment of rents and other dues, they were of some degree of importance to the national coffers, even if not at the same level as grain and cattle.

CHAPTER 19

Some Hae Meat

The growth of the cattle trade with England around 1700 led to massive southward movement of animals on the hoof, along an intricate network of droving tracks. What effect did this have on the meat trade of earlier days, and what was the nature of that trade?

Clues can be got by looking at the nature of animal products that were exported. Between 1550 and 1625, for example, the total export of hides and sheepskins has been estimated at half-a-million a year. Tallow was also a frequent export item. The slaughtering of animals for hides, for the harder pieces of fat to melt down for tallow, and the entrails and stomach for puddings, meant that large amounts of raw meat also had to be dealt with, if the exercise was not to be wasteful.

In the towns, fleshers or butchers were active at all levels, and some were men of importance, master butchers to kings and queens. The royal households could pick and process the best. It is

A pig that has been slaughtered, bled, scalded and scraped. At Greenlaw, Berwickshire. Per J. Cowe. C2055.

163

G

Pork hams wrapped in cloth, on the kitchen roof at Turnabrane, Glenesk, Angus. AF, 1967. 53.15.15.

not certain if there were any slaughterhouses as such, though in the 'flesh-houses' butchers had stands where the meat was cut into legs and shoulders and other pieces for sale in the local 'flesh markets'.

The trade was well-organised. There were flesh-pricers, who fixed meat prices. Stances in the markets paid different dues according to whether they were selling lamb, veal, beef or mutton. There were local regulations to prevent the cleaning of entrails for making puddings near wells or the public water supplies. There was also national interest at times. Parliament was concerned about the dearth and scarcity of all kinds of flesh in the 1590s, and the fact that butchers were prohibited in 1561 from slaughtering lambs for three years must surely point to a bad period for the country's sheep and consequently for supplies of mutton and wool.

There was evidently a lively trade in whole carcases at markets. Whether slaughtered 'to landward' or in the burgh, carcases brought to market were expected to have the hides or skins with them, according to sixteenth-century regulations for both Glasgow and Edinburgh. No doubt cheating of various kinds went on, but what seems certain is that slaughtering for the sale of fresh meat in markets could not have been done at any great distance from the markets. Since these were concentrated in burghs, the consumption of fresh meat with any degree of regularity is likely to have been limited to burghs and their immediate vicinity. This is not to say that everyone, high or low, ate meat daily or even once a week in such areas, but it was available if they could afford it.

Beyond the burghs and their hinterlands, the main centres of meat consumption were the estate headquarters, and the abbeys whose numerous fast days presumably made them consumers on a smaller scale. Records of major establishments, and testamentary inventories in the sixteenth and seventeenth centuries, frequently mention beef stands, beef tubs and cauldrons, a 'great beef pot', a skink pot, and the like. Beyond question, a great deal of meat was consumed at higher social levels, in ecclesiastical institutions, and by the army and navy. The sources of supply were through rents and teinds, and through herds of cattle which could be looked after by professional cattlemen known from the fifteenth century as bowmen. The herd of cattle, especially cows, was the bow. The degree of organisation was evidently considerable, for the cows grazed on their own stretches of pasture, the bowgangs, and, as at Coupar Abbey, could shelter in byres or bowhouses when need arose. This is clearly part of the estate organisation that went alongside, but was not part of, the tenant-farming community system, except where a tenant occupied his piece of land in exchange for looking after the herd.

There were times of plenty, and even surfeits, of fresh meat at the times of slaughter. However, the greater part of the meat of cattle, sheep, pig or goat was preserved in some way for later domestic use or for trading purposes. It was a widespread custom to try to lay in what was called a mart in every household, if it could afford one at all, and if not, a number of families would join together in buying one. This was an ox or cow fattened for slaughter around November, perhaps when their working lives as draught animals and calf producers were done. Marts were frequently included in payments of rent or other dues in kind, whole or in half units or less. No doubt many small farmers had a struggle to produce this requirement, which was meat they would never eat themselves. If a cattle beast could not be afforded, meat of some other kind could be used, such as mutton, or goat's flesh, which some called the 'poor man's mart', or pork; but beef was the preferred meat.

The carcase, cut into pieces, was cured by pickling and salting in barrels, and stored for use. Obviously, even a whole ox, not to mention a part of one, or smaller animals, would by no means provide meat daily for a whole family for any length of time. Such fine things were reserved for Yuletide and special occasions.

There were other ways of curing meat, as well as fish. To ham was to cure the hindquarters of beef, pork or mutton by salting and smoking, a practice formerly known in the Borders and South-West. To reest was to cure by drying and smoking, which was no problem in farm kitchens with a central hearth, or inside one of the bigger 'hanging chimneys'. For this, no salt was needed. However, salting was the commonest medium, for home use and for trade, and even in the 1690s it appears that beef was salted in cows' hides in the Western Isles, carried to Glasgow, and there barrelled and exported to the West Indies.

From quite early on, there was evidently a trade in calves, which provided skins from which soft gloves could be made, and veal. As with cattle, sources of supply were of both high and low social level. On estates or monastic lands there were professional calfherds, and there were special places, calf wards, for looking after them. In the far West, and no doubt elsewhere, calves had to be killed in summer to lessen the number for rearing and conserve scarce grazing resources, especially for overwintering. It is for this kind of reason that veal often appeared in the markets.

To such sources of meat could be added poultry and rabbits, as well as game, but it is fairly certain that regular meat-eating was for long a mark of social status. Poorer people ate meat when they could, particularly on rare festive occasions. On the dinner table at Brahan Castle near Dingwall in the 1780s there was not only an abundance of fish, fowl and poultry, but also beef, mutton, veal, lamb, pork, venison and hare. All of these were on the table at the same time. The tenants around would only have had their potatoes, and their oatmeal and milk dishes, and fish from time to time; or they might have bled their cows once or twice a year, boiled the blood, thickened it with oatmeal, and eaten it in dishes with a little milk. As a writer in 1750 observed, 'this was food I did not admire'.

It was long before the regular eating of meat spread to the lower levels of society. Even in the 1840s, it was still only the wealthier tradesmen who ate butcher meat regularly, though by this time it was beginning to be more widespread. One example of the spread

Rabbits in East Lothian in the 1690s, a regular source of extra meat.
From Slezer, *Theatrum Scotiae*, 1693. LIB/1567.

was the custom that developed about then of the keeping of pigs by
farm servants, especially in South and East-Central Scotland. A
piglet bought in April would be fat for slaughter the following
winter, at the age of six months to a year. Then followed the
business of scalding with boiling water to loosen the bristles and
let them be scraped off, before the pig was hung from a gambrel
and disembowelled. After it had been cut into pieces, wet or dry
curing was done, in a brine keg, or by rubbing with dry salt. There
was no part of the pig that was not used, except, as people said, its
squeak.

Scotland is a maritime country with a great stretch of coastline.
Inevitably, fish was a major element in the diet of the coastal zones,
though in salted form it could travel far inland. Salt herring was
the main traveller. By the 1840s it seems to have been more
common amongst country folk than earlier on, perhaps because it
made a good accompaniment to the potato. In the 1860s, dried or
salt herring was an element in the diet of farmworkers in most
counties, usually for dinner or supper, but in Midlothian and
Lanarkshire also for breakfast. In New Deer, Aberdeenshire, it was

A butcher in Arbroath, about 1915. Per Bruce Walker. C2014.

said about this time that farmworkers fared poorly, and could only afford a barrel of the cheaper herrings, which was no doubt their form of 'poor man's mart'. This was eaten with potatoes for dinner by the head of the household.

Where fishing was carried on as a commercial venture, the bigger fish caught in boats offshore were processed for sale, and though some no doubt found their way into hungry stomachs, local folk had in the main to depend on an age-old form of fishing from the rocks of the shore. In the Northern and Western Isles, the kind of fish caught was mainly coalfish, using a rod and line, or a circular net raised and lowered on a pole. The young fish, called sillocks or piltocks or cuddies, provided oil for lamps as well as food. For several months of the year, such fish in dried or salted form was really a substitute for cereal-based dishes, eaten with milk and potatoes if these could be got.

In fresh water, trout and salmon are the prerogatives of estates or others who have come to own the rights, and can be fished for by those prepared to pay rent for a stretch of river for a season. These and other fish were at home on the tables of higher-class houses. Judging from the amount of poaching equipment in museums and private collections, items such as iron multi-pronged salmon

The island of Boreray, a rich source of wild fowl for the St. Kildans. AF, 1970s. 53.10.12

leisters and ingenious wooden otters that can carry a line with a set of hooks well out into the centre of a loch, a good deal must have found its way into humbler stomachs also. The old story about farm servants bargaining with their masters not to have too much salmon in their diet is one of the pieces of popular culture that regularly finds its way into the pages of local papers and magazines. The truth of it may never be established, but generally speaking, fish of any kind was eaten when possible, as a highlight in the routine of milk and meal-based dishes.

Domestic poultry, and especially hens and geese, were commonly included as part of rent paid in kind, either directly, or as eggs and feathers. Well-known fowling cliffs like those in the islands of St Kilda and of Orkney and Shetland helped also to pay the rents of indwellers.

Geese were widely kept, and in areas like the Northern Isles they seem to have been the main source of poultry meat. In 1792, 4,424 lbs. of goose-feathers, 240 smoked geese and 10 barrels of salted geese were exported from Stromness in Orkney. The geese were treated like cattle. They were herded on the common grazings where they had little huts of stone or turf. Those that were sitting on eggs had the special privilege of sharing the farm kitchens, many of which had recesses in the walls for this purpose.

Hens, on the other hand, mostly stayed about the houses, roosting on spars in the byre until the time when hen-houses began to be prominent in the early 1900s. Though farmers tended to regard them as a nuisance, and often forbade their cotters to keep them, nevertheless by the late eighteenth century stone hen-houses were being included in the steadings of improved farms. At the same time, in the South-East, there appeared a form of organised collecting and marketing arrangement for eggs. The middlemen were egglers, hawkers who travelled on foot, gathering surplus eggs from farmers, hinds and shepherds, and carrying them in creels to their markets. Glasgow's demands for food led to a similar egg trade with the Western Isles after the 1840s. In Skye, for example, women went around exchanging groceries, tea or tobacco for eggs, and sent them in boxes by steamboat to Glasgow.

The eggs of wild fowl were much eaten, where they were available. Gulls, fulmars, puffins, razorbills, guillemots etc. all paid tribute in eggs harvested from their nests in the month of May. Guillemot and gannet flesh was eaten. The inhabitants of Ness still go annually to Sula Sgeir for gannets to be salted, but for organised farming of the fowling cliffs, St Kilda was unique. The year's cycle was killing of gannets and some shearwaters in April; collecting the eggs of puffins and catching fulmars in May; snaring puffins in July; catching fulmars and gannets in August; and catching young gannets in September.

But these activities, including the use of the produce of the cliffs in paying rents, were a response to an extreme environment. Elsewhere, wild birds and their eggs were welcome supplements to the diet, rather than a major focus of economic activity.

CHAPTER 20

Our Daily Bread

As long as the wages of farm servants were paid entirely or partly in kind, there was a close relationship between food and wages. Married workers in the late 1600s had allowances that included, for example, oats and pease, with pieces of ground to sow oats and bere, and a kailyard for kail and other greens. Unmarried workers boarded in the farmhouse would have shared in the food the family ate, and got part of their wage in money. The range of diet for farmers' families and farm servants probably did not differ very much at this period, being based on the produce of the soil (oats, bere, pease, beans) and of the cows (milk, butter, cheese), with meat and fish only occasionally. However, coarser bread or oatcakes were sometimes baked for servants.

On any farm, preserved stores, to keep up supplies for family and servants, took up a good deal of space. The testament of a Selkirkshire farmer, drawn up in 1745, included two meal arks,

The morning brose at Gormyre Farm, Torphichen, West Lothian. Per A. R. Jones. C1123.

three tubs, a flesh boat, four butter kits, three cogs, six milk bowies, two stoups, two kail pots and a kettle, a brass pan, a salt vat, a brander, a girdle, a sowens sieve, a baking board, a meal container of straw, two basins, a pewter stoup and jug, six pewter plates, three trenchers and a dish of earthenware, eleven wooden trenchers, six plates, six wooden bowls, twelve horn spoons, eight pewter spoons, six dozen bottles, a crook and clips for hanging pots over the fire, a pair of tongs and a flesh hook. He had almost no earthenware utensils, and there is no reference to knives or forks. Cereal and milk products were the main stored items.

The farmer here had three male and three female servants. In a later description of the same kitchen, the goodman sat at the end of a long table with his wife and family next to him. The servants were at the end farthest from the window. At dinner, broth was served in large wooden bowls and supped with the horn spoons. This could be followed by a piece of boiled meat, put before the farmer and carved by him for the rest with a clasped knife and fork that he always carried with him. The distributed meat was eaten with the fingers. Even as late as the 1840s in Berwickshire, and no doubt elsewhere, servants remembered how the master shared out butcher meat for the rest to eat with their fingers. Finally, the broth was replaced on the table and supped along with barley bannocks. Meat was not eaten daily by any means; at other times, cheese, butter, milk, salt herrings or oatmeal dumplings took its place.

On this Selkirk farm, family and servants dined together, even if separated at table. One of the noticeable aspects of the Improvement period, and of the new farmhouses whose room layout reflected a separation of functions that had earlier characterised the higher classes, was a growing degree of separation between farmers and servants. Farmhouses became separate from steadings, and servant accommodation began to be a little way off also. The new day was bringing with it new social standards amongst farm folk in the main farming areas. The changes were done quite consciously, in order, as was said in Fife about 1800, to 'put an end to that indiscriminate intercourse in respect of sitting and eating, which was common in former times'. In general, the separatist movement was well on its way by 1750, though sometimes old habits can die hard. One small laird in Peeblesshire always dined with his servants, until he married a second wife. She was conscious of prestige, and a compromise had to be worked out: he took tea for

(Left) Baking oatcakes on a kitchen range at Pitglassie Smithy, Auchterless, Aberdeenshire. There is a toaster in front for hardening off the 'quarters'. AF, 1960. 53.15.19. (Right) Baking round oatcake 'bannocks' at Turnabrane, Glenesk, Angus. The large, semicircular toaster sits on the floor. AF, 1967. 53.15.17.

breakfast with his wife in the parlour, and ate his porridge afterwards with the servants in the kitchen. Some parish ministers deplored the move of the servants away from the family table with the man of the house presiding, for 'his presence and conversation produced the most beneficial effects on the manners and morals of the domestics'. In reality, there may not have been much to choose between them. Be that as it may, the togetherness of pre-Improvement days had gone forever.

The change had a considerable effect on diet. Single men, formerly boarded in the households, were moved to bothies, where they looked after themselves. There was sometimes an in-between stage in the 1790s when farmers' wives prepared the servants' food with their own, but that did not last long, and an allowance of victuals was given instead. The typical situation in the Carse of Gowrie, a major bothy area, was that the men got an English pint of milk daily, or two pints of buttermilk, for breakfast, dinner and supper, with thirty-six ounces of oatmeal per man, along with salt or 1/- in lieu. As a result, the unmarried ploughmen and farm lads ate oatmeal with milk three times a day. The preferred dish was brose, made simply and easily by pouring boiling water onto oatmeal in a wooden bowl, adding a little salt, and eating it with milk.

Though oatmeal had always been a major item in the Scottish diet, there had never been a time when it was used as exclusively as in the bothy men's diet. This was true of others also. A *Report on the Dietaries of Scotch Agricultural Labourers* in 1869 claimed that oatmeal formed the main article of daily subsistence among 90% of working-class families. Some variety was possible in the better bothies, as in an Angus one in 1813 where breakfast was porridge or brose, dinner of oatcakes with butter or skimmed milk, cheese and milk, and supper of sowens (flummery, made from the fine dust of meal) or potatoes. All the same, oatmeal was the major element. There is no hint of meat in the diet of bothy men.

This concentration on oatmeal in the bothies is a special case, one of the outcomes of the agricultural revolution. But what was the more general situation regarding cereal crops?

For most of Scotland, the main crops were oats and bere or barley. By the late 1600s, as a result of liming on the outfield, the acreage of oats had begun to expand. This had an adverse effect on the consumption of bere. Bere continued as a major constituent of broth, and as the basis for brewing ale, but as bread and bannocks and bere-meal it was falling out of favour in the Lowlands by that date. This may have been partly a result of the same kind of social differentiation as was noted in Caithness in 1812: for the farmer's family, fine bere-meal scones were made at sixteen to the pound of meal, whilst the servants were given thicker scones of more coarsely ground meal.

Oatmeal took the place of bere-meal, except amongst the poorer classes. In the Highlands, however, bere was not replaced by oats to the same extent, and bannocks of bere-meal and bere-meal porridge were being widely eaten there well through the nineteenth century. In fact, bere-meal scones and bannocks are still eaten on the farms and crofts of Caithness and Orkney and can be bought in the bakers' shops there.

It is a curious aspect of human nature that when a food declines in the social scale, it can sometimes return as a prestige element in the diet, or as a health food. The Caithness distinction in grades in

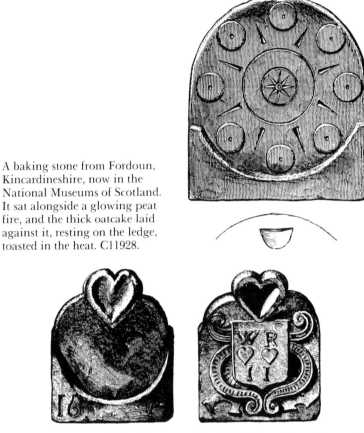

A baking stone from Fordoun, Kincardineshire, now in the National Museums of Scotland. It sat alongside a glowing peat fire, and the thick oatcake laid against it, resting on the ledge, toasted in the heat. C11928.

The back and front of a baking-stone dated 1674, from Clova, Angus. In Dundee Museum. C11929.

1812 shows two levels of normal use. In Perthshire in the 1790s, bere-bannocks were the common bread of the Highlanders, those of middle rank ate oatcakes, and on the tables of the upper classes twice-shelled and refined barley cakes were to be seen. Already in the Borders in the early 1700s, bere-meal porridge was thought good for the health of ladies and for schoolchildren, which implies that even then it was not especially regarded as a man's food. At all events, in the form of baked products and porridge, it was well on its way out by about 1800 in the Lowlands.

For the last two centuries, the eating of oatmeal has been seen as a mark of Scottish identity. There is no doubt, however, that it came much more into fashion in the eighteenth century, as bere lost face and as the acreage of oats increased. It was a major item in the meals of nearly all classes, as can be seen from a description of a typical North-East farmer's daily fare in 1782. Meat, incidentally, was never eaten except at baptisms and weddings, and at Christmas and on Shrove Tuesday. Breakfast was of porridge eaten with milk or ale, or brose made with the liquid from boiled cabbage or kail left overnight. This was followed by oatcakes and milk. If milk was scarce, ale or small beer was the substitute. For dinner, there was sowens eaten with milk, followed by oatcakes with milk or kail. Supper was of two courses during winter, of kail-brose, eaten about 7 pm, and then kail eaten with oatcakes, about 9 pm. In summer, one course was the rule, of porridge and milk, or oatcakes and kail, or milk. These meals were common to the family and servants. Dependence on oatmeal, milk and the produce of the kailyard was almost total.

Other areas had other fashions. About the same date in Ross-shire, workers maintained in the family were given two meals a day. They started work at 4 or 5 am, breakfasted at 11 am, had dinner at 3 pm, and stopped work at 7 or 8 pm. Sowens were eaten for dinner, and if it happened that a third meal was allowed, it was a thin gruel of oatmeal, brochan, with bere-meal bread. This appears to be extremely spartan.

In Orkney, work hours were equally long. The morning piece at 3 am was a bite of bere-meal bread and a drink of buttermilk. Breakfast at 8 am was of boiled sowens or porridge, with a bowl of milk. Dinner was at 3 or 4 pm, of fish or potatoes boiled in one pot, or pork and kail, or potatoes and herring. Work ended at 7 or 8 pm and supper followed, with mashed potatoes and milk, or kail and potatoes, or kail and dehusked barley. Orkney seems to have been a land of plenty, though it must be understood that this was the regime on bigger places.

Farther south, in Perth, breakfast was of porridge or brose with skimmed milk or ale; dinner of water kail, i.e. a broth of green kail and other vegetables and field pease and groats, sometimes with nettles being used as greens, eaten with pease bannocks; supper was of sowens or brose.

In Roxburgh, the diet of married servants was bread, oatmeal, potatoes, milk, cheese, eggs, herring and salt meat. The bread was of barley- or pease-meal, kneaded into bannocks and toasted over a fire. Oatcakes were similarly toasted, but were much thinner. House-servants had breakfast of oatmeal porridge or sowens with milk; dinner of broth and boiled meat warm twice a week, or of re-heated broth, or milk, with cold meat, or eggs, cheese, butter and bread of mixed barley- and pease-meal; supper was as for breakfast, or in winter there could be boiled potatoes mashed with a little butter and milk.

The greater variety appears to have lain in Orkney and Roxburgh, at opposite ends of the country. The Roxburgh situation was a reflection of the eating system across the Border. In between, however, there was a more uniform level of use of the 'standard' dietary ingredients, meal, milk and kail, with potatoes gradually creeping in. The 1869 *Report on the Dietaries of Scotch Agricultural Labourers* commented on this very degree of uniformity. To a great extent, especially in the farming zones, it resulted from the social differentiation between farmers and servants as the course of Improvement went on.

Kail as a major source of greens was one of the most important plants grown around the houses. From at least the 1400s, various types of Brassica were grown and eaten in a variety of ways. Sometimes it was eaten alone, boiled and mashed with the addition of butter, milk, salt and pepper if available. More often it was combined with a cereal, especially bere or barley, in the form of kail-broth, or as a base for making brose or a kind of porridge. A piece of salt meat might be laid on top.

Kail was one of the most common elements in the diet of the farming communities. Few Scots would not have had some experience of the frightful smell of burned kail when the pot went dry. The language of everyday was full of proverbs and sayings about kail. The word came to be used not only for the plant, but also for broth made from it, and even for the main meal itself. 'To earn salt to your kail' was to be able to make a livelihood.

Though bere and oats were the most widespread cereal crops in Scotland, the crop that was most valuable in itself was wheat. It was grown as the main cash crop in the best farming areas, i.e. the South-East, the Carse of Gowrie, the Laigh of Moray, and parts of Fife and Easter Ross. The growing of wheat marked the richer centres from which agricultural improvements spread.

Throughout the country, the form of 'bread' that was normally eaten was of bere-meal and oatmeal, and flat in shape. This was true even in the wheat-growing districts, for the crop was for sale, and not for everyday baking purposes. The open hearths of rural buildings were suited to baking flat bread on iron girdles or gridded branders, but had no ovens for the baking of loaf bread.

Ovens were to be found in towns and in castles and mansions. They were rare elsewhere. They ensured that the higher classes had regular supplies of white or wheaten bread, and that it was available for those in towns and cities who could afford it. Until the eighteenth century and often much later, it was rare for folk in country districts to taste it.

There was one exception to the rule. The eagerness of farmers to have their crops harvested quickly and efficiently seems to have encouraged them to treat the workers particularly well at shearing time, whether they were part of the standard labour force or seasonal migrants. The food provided then was better than the ordinary fare. In the 1790s, wheat bread with ale was given for the supper and dinner of shearers in Berwickshire, and for the breakfast and dinner of those in Angus. Twelve loaves, baked from 8 lbs. of flour, provided breakfast for twelve Angus shearers. The loaves were 10⅔ oz. each. Shearers in Roxburgh got a 20 oz. loaf of coarse wheat with a bottle of small beer for dinner. Loaves could vary in size, evidently, for in sixteenth-century Moray weights of 22 oz. are mentioned. A loaf of such a size was regarded as a meal in itself, and this is confirmed by the contemporary manuscript Old Cambus Accounts in Berwickshire, which record the baking of white bread with eggs for the supper and dinner of servants who had travelled some distance.

By the end of the first decade of the nineteenth century, the use of wheat bread was increasing, and farmers in Angus were said to have started keeping a proportion of the second-quality wheat to be ground into flour for the baking of scones. Without ovens, they could not bake it into loaves, except occasionally by using a pot oven. However, the farther from the wheat-growing areas and towns, the more dependent people were on local produce. In Caithness in 1812, it was said that although the upper classes ate as well as in South Scotland, nevertheless oatmeal or barley-meal cakes were used instead of wheaten bread. Even so, change was close, for a baker in Thurso and another in Wick had just started to import wheaten flour.

Town bakery and delivery vans, in Inverness. Per Mrs Skinner, via Inverness Museum. C5486.

Clearly, white bread was for long an upper-class food that began to be more widespread at lower social levels in the course of the nineteenth century, though known at these levels before then at festival occasions and as a major part of the diet during shearing. The spread in its use took place first in the towns, where by the early 1800s — at least in East Lothian — it was mostly wheat bread that was eaten. Bakers' shops spread rapidly also. Wigtown had one baker in 1755, and four or five in 1795. From such centres the move to the countryside followed, though it was long before farm servants, with their heavy dependence on oatmeal, were able to adopt wheat bread as a regular element in their diet.

What were the alternatives to wheat bread? The main crops were bere and oats, and pease and beans also have to be reckoned with, though mainly in the Lowlands. Both pease-meal and bean-meal bread were made. Bere-meal was commonly mixed with a third to a quarter of pease- or bean-meal and baked on an iron girdle with salt and water, but no yeast, into round cakes about an inch thick. Such flat bread could also be baked in front of the fire by leaving it against a baking stone — of which some nicely-carved examples survive — or any other convenient support. In Fife in the 1780s, such mixed bread was being eaten partly by the upper classes and entirely by the lower classes. In Moray, around 1810, bread of bere-meal mixed with bean-, -pease, -rye- or wheat flour was baked in the coastal zone. Inland there was no such mixing and the normal 'bread' was oatcakes, said to be of two thicknesses. Possibly the thinner cakes were baked on a girdle, and the thicker ones against a baking stone.

The mixture of ground cereal grains and legumes was called mashlum and was already known in the fifteenth century, mainly in the farming areas of the East and South, from Cromarty to Galloway. Already by the 1600s there is evidence of social differentiation in the South, for by then the eating of pease-bread or bean-bread, with no admixture of cereal, was confined to poorer people. In some areas, like parts of Perthshire, thin, flaccid bannocks of pease- or bean-meal were being eaten by all classes as late as 1800, although they were becoming rarer by then. The subtle pressures of prestige led to the abandonment of such foods at an earlier date in the more fertile farming areas, though it seems also that a mashlum mixture was being deliberately sown by farmers there, in relatively small quantities, as a crop from which bread could be made for their servants. In this respect also, improvements did not upgrade or diversify the dietary standards of farmworkers.

Junk food of modern days. Young lads eating candy floss at Turriff Agricultural Show. AF, 1986. 51.57.36.

Conclusion

The material looked at in the twenty chapters of this book is concerned with change, before and after 1750, to give a round figure.

Before then, there was a slow but nevertheless persistent movement, so unobtrusive that small clues have to be looked for and put together before we can see that it was happening at all. The preconditions of such change lay in subsistence needs, and the very question of survival itself. A rhythm of life was evolved over long years to turn the resources of the environment into food and warmth, manure and shelter, with just enough of a surplus to cover rents and other recurring dues, and occasional basic essential purchases. It worked, given good weather, peace, a fixed level of population, and demands that were within reason from lords and masters. It failed when these or other pressures upset the balance, which was precarious enough in all conscience. Times of failure speeded up eventual change, much as wartime conditions always do, as the masters tried to reorganise so that the resources that were most valuable to them, land and manpower, should not be wasted. However, as long as the old community persisted, with its quite highly evolved and specific rhythms, there were serious limits to reorganisation. Areas under cultivation could be extended to take account of growing populations, and more intensive use could be made of upland grazings, but the options were few. There is little doubt that by the middle of the eighteenth century the taking up of slack on available options had gone as far as it could, at least in the Lowland farming areas.

Before 1750, change had an evolutionary character. After that date, the change was much more like a revolution in nature. It was, of course, organised from above. National enabling legislation had been passed already in the second half of the seventeenth century, and was later implemented at estate or barony level. The period of what we call the Agricultural Revolution was beyond doubt a deliberate affair. It also had a quality of inevitability about it, when masters and men came to be swept along on a tide they could not stem. If they could not stem it, they had to learn to control it. They did so in ways described or touched on in this book: reorganising the farming landscape, setting up villages where domestic industries were practised, fostering such industries (especially textiles), exploiting local mineral resources in coal, lime and lead, and natural resources like seaweed for kelp-burning, making use of water power in the countryside, commercialising the grazing resources of Highland areas, and erecting buildings that reflected the new view of farming as an industry.

It could be said that the old way of life was replaced by business attitudes. It would be trite to do so, for the Revolution led to the evolution of new ways of life. For many, there was very severe disruption of the deep-ingrained rhythms of centuries. It is a task of the future to consider what psychological problems this may have led to, and certainly there are data enough on the displaced persons of more recent days to provide clues to the atmosphere of two centuries ago, when the roots of all aspects of the modern world were being planted.

The countryside did settle down again. New routines were established. New tools and equipment and housing, stock-breeding and plant-propagation, carried Scottish farming to high levels of attainment which were widely influential. Living standards and life expectancy improved, so that sons could take it for granted, almost for the first time in human existence, that they would know their own grandparents.

As long as horses provided motive power, the new rhythms of work and life continued, creating a world of horseman's word and bothy ballad, and of man and master relationships in a situation where the master was both the employer of men and also the tenant responsible for paying the rent. A cosy, familiar form of working within the organisation of the estate grew and remained, till the tractor opened the way to newer farming technology, whose needs are in turn bringing to an end the usefulness of farm buildings and farm systems that have served us well for two hundred years. A new revolution is at hand.

Lowsin' time for dinner, in 1907, at Carriston farm, Markinch, Fife. Per
A. Barron. C7477.

Suggested Further Reading

For those who wish to read more about the questions raised in this book, the following sources can be recommended:

J. T. Coppock. *An Agricultural Atlas of Scotland*, Edinburgh 1976.

T. M. Devine, ed., *Farm Servants and Labour in Lowland Scotland*, Edinburgh 1984.

A. Fenton, *Scottish Country Life*, Edinburgh 1976, reprinted 1977. A full bibliography is included.

A. Fenton, *The Island Blackhouse*, HMSO 1978.

A. Fenton, *The Shape of the Past*, 2 vols., Edinburgh 1986.

A Fenton and B. Walker, *The Rural Architecture of Scotland*, Edinburgh 1981.

J. Hunter, *The Making of the Crofting Community*, Edinburgh 1976.

R. S. Morton, *Traditional Farm Architecture in Scotland*, Edinburgh 1976.

R. J. Naismith, *Buildings of the Scottish Countryside*, London 1985.

W. Orr, *Deer Forests, Landlords and Crofters*, Edinburgh 1982.

M. L. Parry and T. R. Slater, eds., *The Making of the Scottish Countryside*, London & Montreal, 1980.

M. H. B. Sanderson, *Scottish Rural Society in the Sixteenth Century*, Edinburgh 1982.

T. C. Smout, *A Century of the Scottish People, 1830-1950*, London 1986.

I. Whyte, *Agriculture and Society in Seventeenth-Century Scotland*, Edinburgh 1979.

Index and Glossary

talk about action. It is a blind thing dependent
on external influences, and moved by an impulse
of whose nature it is unconscious. It is a thing in-
complete in its essence, because limited by accident,
and ignorant of its direction, being always at variance
with its aim. Its basis is the lack of imagination.
It is the last resource of those who know not how
to dream.

Ernest. Gilbert, you treat the world as if it were
a crystal ball. You hold it in your hand, and reverse
it to please a wilful fancy. You do nothing but re-
write history.

Gilbert. The one duty we owe to history is to re-
write it. That is not the least of the tasks in store
for the critical spirit. When we have fully discovered
the scientific laws that govern life, we shall realize
that the one person who has more illusions than the
dreamer is the man of action. He, indeed, knows
neither the origin of his deeds nor their results.
From the field in which he thought that he had
sown thorns, we have gathered our vintage, and the
fig-tree that he planted for our pleasure is as barren
as the thistle, and more bitter. It is because
Humanity has never known where it was going that
it has been able to find its way.

Ernest. You think, then, that in the sphere of
action a conscious aim is a delusion?

parallels of thought-movement may be traced in the
Anthology, American journalism, to which no parallel can be found anywhere, and the ballad in sham
Scotch dialect, which one of our most industrious
writers has recently proposed should be made the
basis for a final and unanimous effort on the part of
our second-rate poets to make themselves really
romantic. Each new school, as it appears, cries out
against criticism, but it is to the critical faculty in
man that it owes its origin. The mere creative
instinct does not innovate, but reproduces.

Ernest. You have been talking of criticism as an
essential part of the creative spirit, and I now fully
accept your theory. But what of criticism outside
creation? I have a foolish habit of reading periodi-
cals, and it seems to me that most modern criticism
is perfectly valueless.

Gilbert. So is most modern creative work also.
Mediocrity weighing mediocrity in the balance, and
incompetence applauding its brother—that is the
spectacle which the artistic activity of England
affords us from time to time. And yet, I feel I am
a little unfair in this matter. As a rule, the critics—
I speak, of course, of the higher class, of those in
fact who write for the sixpenny papers—are far
more cultured than the people whose work they are
called upon to review. This is, indeed, only what

one would expect, for criticism demands infinitely more cultivation than creation does.

Ernest. Really?

Gilbert. Certainly. Anybody can write a three-volumed novel. It merely requires a complete ignorance of both life and literature. The difficulty that I should fancy the reviewer feels is the difficulty of sustaining any standard. Where there is no style a standard must be impossible. The poor reviewers are apparently reduced to be the reporters of the police-court of literature, the chroniclers of the doings of the habitual criminals of art. It is sometimes said of them that they do not read all through the works they are called upon to criticise. They do not. Or at least they should not. If they did so, they would become confirmed misanthropes, or if I may borrow a phrase from one of the pretty Newnham graduates, confirmed womanthropes for the rest of their lives. Nor is it necessary. To know the vintage and quality of a wine one need not drink the whole cask. It must be perfectly easy in half an hour to say whether a book is worth anything or worth nothing. Ten minutes are really sufficient, if one has the instinct for form. Who wants to wade through a dull volume? One tastes it, and that is quite enough—more than enough, I should imagine. I am aware that there are many

honest workers in painting as well who object to criticism entirely. right. Their work stands in no intel to their age. It brings us no ne pleasure. It suggests no fresh depart or passion, or beauty. It should no It should be left to the oblivion that

Ernest. But, my dear fellow—excu rupting you—you seem to me to be passion for criticism to lead you a gre For, after all, even you must admit t more difficult to do a thing than to ta

Gilbert. More difficult to do a thin about it? Not at all. That is a error. It is very much more difficult thing than to do it. In the sphere of is of course obvious. Anybody can Only a great man can write it. The of action, no form of emotion, that we with the lower animals. It is only by we rise above them, or above each o guage, which is the parent, and not thought. Action, indeed, is always e presented to us in its most aggravated, continuous form, which I take to be tl dustry, becomes simply the refuge o have nothing whatsoever to do. No,

Gilbert. It is worse than a delusion.   If we lived long enough to see the results of our actions it may be that those who call themselves good would be sickened with a dull remorse, and those whom the world calls evil stirred by a noble joy.   Each little thing that we do passes into the great machine of life, which may grind our virtues to powder and make them worthless, or transform our sins into elements of a new civilization, more marvellous and more splendid than any that has gone before.   But men are the slaves of words.   They rage against Materialism, as they call it, forgetting that there has been no material improvement that has not spiritualized the world, and that there have been few, if any, spiritual awakenings that have not wasted the world's faculties in barren hopes, and fruitless aspirations, and empty or trammelling creeds.   What is termed Sin is an essential element of progress.   Without it the world would stagnate, or grow old, or become colourless.   By its curiosity, Sin increases the experience of the race.   Through its intensified assertion of individualism, it saves us from monotony of type.   In its rejection of the current notions about morality, it is one with the higher ethics.   And as for the virtues!   What are the virtues?   Nature, M. Renan tells us, cares little about chastity, and it may be that it is to the shame of the Magdalen, and

not to their own purity, that the Lucretias of
modern life owe their freedom from stain. Charity,
as even those of whose religion it makes a formal
part have been compelled to acknowledge, creates
a multitude of evils. The mere existence of conscience, that faculty of which people prate so much
nowadays, and are so ignorantly proud, is a sign of
our imperfect development. It must be merged in
instinct before we become fine. Self-denial is simply
a method by which man arrests his progress, and
self-sacrifice a survival of the mutilation of the
savage, part of that old worship of pain which is so
terrible a factor in the history of the world, and
which even now makes its victims day by day, and
has its altars in the land. Virtues! Who knows
what the virtues are? Not you. Not I. Not anyone. It is well for our vanity that we slay the
criminal, for if we suffered him to live he might
show us what we had gained by his crime. It is
well for his peace that the saint goes to his martyr-
dom. He is spared the sight of the horror of his
harvest.

Ernest. Gilbert, you sound too harsh a note. Let
us go back to the more gracious fields of literature.
What was it you said?   That it was more difficult to
talk about a thing than to do it?

Gilbert (*after a pause*). Yes: I believe I ventured

upon that simple truth. Surely you see now that I
am right? When man acts he is a puppet. When
he describes he is a poet. The whole secret lies in
that. It was easy enough on the sandy plains by
windy Ilion to send the notched arrow from the
painted bow, or to hurl against the shield of hide
and flame-like brass the long ash-handled spear. It
was easy for the adulterous queen to spread the
Tyrian carpets for her lord, and then, as he lay
couched in the marble bath, to throw over his head
the purple net, and call to her smooth-faced lover to
stab through the meshes at the heart that should have
broken at Aulis. For Antigone even, with Death
waiting for her as her bridegroom, it was easy to pass
through the tainted air at noon, and climb the hill,
and strew with kindly earth the wretched naked
corse that had no tomb. But what of those who
wrote about these things? What of those who gave
them reality, and made them live for ever? Are
they not greater than the men and women they sing
of? " Hector that sweet knight is dead," and Lu-
cian tells us how in the dim underworld Menippus
saw the bleaching skull of Helen, and marvelled that
it was for so grim a favour that all those horned ships
were launched, those beautiful mailed men laid low,
those towered cities brought to dust. Yet, every
day the swan-like daughter of Leda comes out on the

battlements, and looks down at the tide of war. The
greybeards wonder at her loveliness, and she stands
by the side of the king. In his chamber of stained
ivory lies her leman. He is polishing his dainty
armour, and combing the scarlet plume. With
squire and page, her husband passes from tent to
tent. She can see his bright hair, and hears, or fan-
cies that she hears, that clear cold voice. In the
courtyard below, the son of Priam is buckling on his
brazen cuirass. The white arms of Andromache are
around his neck. He sets his helmet on the ground,
lest their babe should be frightened. Behind the
embroidered curtains of his pavilion sits Achilles,
in perfumed raiment, while in harness of gilt and silver the friend of his soul arrays himself to go forth
to the fight. From a curiously carven chest that his
mother Thetis had brought to his ship-side, the Lord
of the Myrmidons takes out that mystic chalice that
the lip of man had never touched, and cleanses it
with brimstone, and with fresh water cools it, and,
having washed his hands, fills with black wine its
burnished hollow, and spills the thick grape-blood
upon the ground in honour of Him whom at Dodona
barefooted prophets worshipped, and prays to Him,
and knows not that he prays in vain, and that by the
hands of two knights from Troy, Panthous' son,
Euphorbus, whose love-locks were looped with gold,

and the Priamid, the lion-hearted, Patroklus, the comrade of comrades, must meet his doom. Phantoms, are they? Heroes of mist and mountain? Shadows in a song? No: they are real. Action! What is action? It dies at the moment of its energy. It is a base concession to fact. The world is made by the singer for the dreamer.

Ernest. While you talk it seems to me to be so.

Gilbert. It is so in truth. On the mouldering citadel of Troy lies the lizard like a thing of green bronze. The owl has built her nest in the palace of Priam. Over the empty plain wander shepherd and goatherd with their flocks, and where, on the wine-surfaced, oily sea, οἶνοψ πόντος, as Homer calls it, copper-prowed and streaked with vermilion, the great galleys of the Danaoi came in their gleaming crescent, the lonely tunny-fisher sits in his little boat and watches the bobbing corks of his net. Yet, every morning the doors of the city are thrown open, and on foot, or in horse-drawn chariot, the warriors go forth to battle, and mock their enemies from behind their iron masks. All day long the fight rages, and when night comes the torches gleam by the tents, and the cresset burns in the hall. Those who live in marble or on painted panel, know of life but a single exquisite instant, eternal indeed in its beauty, but limited to one note of passion or one mood of calm.

Those whom the poet makes live have their myriad emotions of joy and terror, of courage and despair, of pleasure and of suffering.   The seasons come and go in glad or saddening pageant, and with winged or leaden feet the years pass by before them.   They have their youth and their manhood, they are children, and they grow old.   It is always dawn for St. Helena, as Veronese saw her at the window. Through the still morning air the angels bring her the symbol of God's pain.   The cool breezes of the morning lift the gilt threads from her brow.   On that little hill by the city of Florence, where the lovers of Giorgione are lying, it is always the solstice of noon, of noon made so languorous by summer suns that hardly can the slim naked girl dip into the marble tank the round bubble of clear glass, and the long fingers of the lute-player rest idly upon the chords. It is twilight always for the dancing nymphs whom Corot set free among the silver poplars of France. In eternal twilight they move, those frail diaphanous figures, whose tremulous white feet seem not to touch the dew-drenched grass they tread on.   But those who walk in epos, drama, or romance, see through the labouring months the young moons wax and wane, and watch the night from evening unto morning star, and from sunrise unto sunsetting can note the shifting day with all its gold and shadow.   For them, as for us, the flowers bloom and wither, and the Earth, that Green-tressed Goddess as Coleridge calls her, alters her raiment for their pleasure. The statue is concentrated to one moment of perfection. The image stained upon the canvas possesses no spiritual element of growth or change. If they know nothing of death, it is because they know little of life, for the secrets of life and death belong to those, and those only, whom the sequence of time affects, and who possess not merely the present but the future, and can rise or fall from a past of glory or of shame. Movement, that problem of the visible arts, can be truly realized by Literature alone. It is Literature that shows us the body in its swiftness and the soul in its unrest.

Ernest. Yes; I see now what you mean. But, surely, the higher you place the creative artist, the lower must the critic rank.

Gilbert. Why so?

Ernest. Because the best that he can give us will be but an echo of rich music, a dim shadow of clear-outlined form. It may, indeed, be that life is chaos, as you tell me that it is; that its martyrdoms are mean and its heroisms ignoble; and that it is the function of Literature to create, from the rough material of actual existence, a new world that will be more marvellous, more enduring, and more true than the world that common eyes look upon, and through which common natures seek to realize their perfection. But surely, if this new world has been made by the spirit and touch of a great artist, it will be a thing so complete and perfect that there will be nothing left for the critic to do. I quite understand now, and indeed admit most readily, that it is far more difficult to talk about a thing than to do it. But it seems to me that this sound and sensible maxim, which is really extremely soothing to one's feelings, and should be adopted as its motto by every Academy of Literature all over the world, applies only to the relations that exist between Art and Life, and not to any relations that there may be between Art and Criticism.

Gilbert. But, surely, Criticism is itself an art. And just as artistic creation implies the working of the critical faculty, and, indeed, without it cannot be said to exist at all, so Criticism is really creative in the highest sense of the word. Criticism is, in fact, both creative and independent.

Ernest. Independent?

Gilbert. Yes; independent. Criticism is no more to be judged by any low standard of imitation or resemblance than is the work of poet or sculptor. The critic occupies the same relation to the work of art that he criticises as the artist does to the visible